I HAVE AUTISM
AND I LIKE TO PLAY
~~GOOD~~ BAD TENNIS

Debashis Paul is a professional management and marketing strategy consultant with clients across New Delhi, Gurgaon, Bengaluru and Kolkata in India, and California in the USA. The lion's share of his present work is for clients in the education sector. He has previously worked in the advertising field with top-notch global advertising agency networks. He has led several integrated pan-India public service campaigns pertaining to critical issues such as malnutrition, malaria and women's health.

He, along with his agency teams, has won many awards for advertising and market effectiveness—national and international (Cannes Lions and New York Festivals).

Outside his profession, one of his interest areas consistently, has been child development psychology—much before he became a dad! Today, he counsels parents who have children with learning and social communication difficulties.

I Have Autism and I Like to Play ~~Good~~ Bad Tennis is the first book he has authored.

PRAISE FOR THE BOOK

'Like the protagonist, this is a gentle book. A father trying to understand his son, to help him find meaning in a confusing world. A warm and refreshing take that all of us could learn from.'

— Merry Barua, *Director, Action for Autism,*
National Centre for Autism, New Delhi

'Kudos to Debashis Paul for this monumental feat! This book was a wonderful read. Very well written, and should be a great resource for parents, particularly in India and South Asia.'

— Dr Kajori Ghosh Thusu, MD,
Paediatrician, California, USA

'This book is written beautifully. This book is for parents to renew their strength and regain their joy.'

— Urooj Hassan, *Autism Parent and Principal,*
Different Not Less School, Lahore

'Heartfelt and moving, Debashis Paul's book is a true celebration of life. This book is a must-read not just for parents but for everyone in order to truly appreciate neurodiversity. Paul not only raises awareness about autism, but shines light on the oft-misunderstood aspects of the condition by sharing his own personal experiences. Intimate and brilliantly written.'

— Sheba Nandkeolyar, *Founder & CEO of MultiConnexions Group,*
President of International Advertising Association Australia Chapter,
National Chair of Australia India Business Council,
Women in Business Chapter, Australia

'The book that Debashis Paul has written about his son, Noel, could have had many titles, but to me it will remain *The Book of*

Unconditional Love. Written with almost scientific precision and the warmest of feelings, this is an exquisite account of living with autism. Paul is unsparing in his honesty throughout the book. He leads us on a journey that is demanding, emotionally draining, intellectually challenging, at times excruciatingly sad, but always beautiful because the writing comes from the heart of a father. Brave and resolute, honest and strong! You will feel you have known both the father and the son, and Noel's wonderful soul will touch your forehead like a gentle breeze from a quiet lake on a summer evening.'

– Dragan Todorovic, Author and Educator,
Centre for Creative Writing, University of Kent, UK

'Debashis Paul has written a very special book from his first-hand experience of loving and raising his son, Noel. With simplicity and elegance, Paul lets us into the world of this magical boy who loves cars and music and makes a case for talking to strangers. Yet the author neither romanticises nor sentimentalises the narrative. The reality of parenting a neurodivergent child is depicted unflinchingly—it is often challenging, even traumatic, but also tremendously beautiful. Written in evocative fragments and with great economy, the book is a gripping read that takes us on a unique journey!'

– Silvija Jestrovic,
Professor, University of Warwick, UK

'Noel Paul lived his father's dream and was indeed "a spreader of joy, one who would embody the values of warm celebration, love, kindness, and togetherness". Debashis has done a brilliant job of giving the reader insights into the world as seen by Noel. Through anecdotes and reminiscences, he has re-created the complex tapestry that is autism. This book is one that parents can turn to for answers, for suggestions, for what works and what does not and most importantly, for hope and for reassurance that the autistic mind is truly beautiful.'

– Sushmita Mitra, Former Head of Special Education,
Vasant Valley School, New Delhi

'This book is a goldmine of insights from a remarkably thoughtful father. Heart-touching. Must read for parents, educators and all who love children.'

– Ranjan Mitter, *Principal,*
The Future Foundation School, Kolkata

'This book is not just another book on autism but an insightful depiction of a human life with a difference. It motivates the reader to appreciate diversity. With this book, Noel becomes my inspiration too and will be one for every reader. A must-read for everyone.'

– Arpita Yadav, *Director, ILP,*
Shaurya Foundation Trust, Palwal, Haryana

DEBASHIS PAUL

I HAVE AUTISM

AND I LIKE TO PLAY ~~GOOD~~ BAD TENNIS

Vignettes and
Insights from My Son's Life

WESTLAND
NON·FICTION

First published by Westland Non-Fiction, an imprint of Westland Books, a division of Nasadiya Technologies Private Limited, in 2023

No. 269/2B, First Floor, 'Irai Arul', Vimalraj Street, Nethaji Nagar, Alapakkam Main Road, Maduravoyal, Chennai 600095

Westland, the Westland logo, Westland Non-Fiction and the Westland Non-Fiction logo are the trademarks of Nasadiya Technologies Private Limited, or its affiliates.

Copyright © Debashis Paul, 2023

Debashis Paul asserts the moral right to be identified as the author of this work.

ISBN: 9789357762816

10 9 8 7 6 5 4 3 2

The views and opinions expressed in this work are the author's own and the facts are as reported by him, and the publisher is in no way liable for the same.

All rights reserved

Typeset by SÜRYA, New Delhi
Printed at Nutech Print Services-India

No part of this book may be reproduced, or stored in a retrieval system, or transmitted in any form or by any means, electronic, mechanical, photocopying, recording, or otherwise, without express written permission of the publisher.

Dedicated to Noel's grandparents, whom he loved and adored.

His Dadu, Utpal Dutt
His Dadabhai, Col. Dr Satya Brata Paul
His Didaan, Sova Sen
His Thamma, Dr Prasadi Paul

Contents

Noel with his Dadu, Utpal Dutt

Foreword

Noel had just turned eighteen when he joined us at the Shaurya Foundation Trust. We had started the vocational training facility for young people with neurological issues. So, in several ways, we grew up together with Noel and, for the most part, he led us on a journey of how to approach, accept and train a person with autism and how to enjoy that person's company. The first lesson we learnt was that autism is a general label and one has to go beyond that label, as each individual is unique and shaped by the sum total of their strengths and experiences in life.

This book will allow the reader a glimpse into Noel's unique strengths and experiences and it will be a great resource for learning parenting and empathy, while engendering respect for another person in the spirit of human inclusiveness.

To say that Debashis is an involved father is surely an understatement. In my long association with parents of persons with disabilities, I have met hundreds of parents—some underestimate, some overestimate, some feel permanently dejected, some disassociate from the child and some make their child the centre of their lives—but there are very few parents and families who enjoy their company and strive to facilitate their independent journey of self-discovery. Debashis is such a father. He and Pia, a remarkable mother, with their lovely daughter, Ahvana, form one such rare family. Noel had the capacity to bring out the best in everyone and as the experiences shared in this book tell us, change does not come overnight; it is an arduous journey filled with disappointments, victories and immense courage that make the magic happen.

My practical experience with autism was limited when I first met Noel and I think that is what enriched my association with him. It was absolutely fascinating and constantly enlightening. The need for structure, logic, routine and pattern was all-pervasive, and what stood out was Noel's warm connection with people. This information is so illuminating and I am sure this book would prove to be a great resource for parents, educators and professionals. It would certainly help build awareness and understanding amongst people at large about autism.

The fact that Noel was verbal provided a lot of clues to what he was experiencing in terms of his moods and anxieties. We, at Shaurya, had a theory that Noel's 'talk' was like an internal dialogue on a loudspeaker—something that offered us clues or codes to understand him better and anticipate his actions. We would work out how to plan the day for Noel by assessing his speech when he arrived at Shaurya—the people, places and incidents he would mention in the first fifteen minutes of arrival would decide our approach towards him for the day. The happy mood days would be super productive. He would invariably talk about going shopping with other students or for an outing to McDonald's. Days when he was in an unhappy mood would be made clear by behaviour, such as letting out shouts of distress, repetitive mentions of breaking a cup or cupping his hands over his ears. Either way, we would gear up to find a productive path forward for this very interesting young man.

He responded wonderfully in individual sessions and always found inventive ways to complete his tasks efficiently. Once, we were working on tying shoelaces and had made elaborate aids to teach Noel. He was not successful initially, so we outlined the task again and left him alone. Voila! he tied the knot using one hand all by himself. Similarly, during the process of making dough balls for the preparation of *mathi*, he used only one hand. Noel's one-handed method led to greater efficiency and proved useful for the other trainees as well. He was always a willing partner in trying new techniques in vocational skill learning.

Noel left us midway, but he guided us in designing the services and in the creation of our independent living facility in Palwal, a residential and skilling campus where each floor has provisions for a 'calming room'—this was all thanks to Noel. He taught us that a safe space is necessary, for an independent living system, to recover when one is overwhelmed and experiencing sensory overload.

Any change is challenging for all of us, but more so for those with autism. This book has multiple examples of how any sudden change can lead to meltdowns and cause immense distress to an autistic person and to their caregivers as well. For instance, during the overnight camps, Noel simply refused to sleep in any of the bedrooms. We had to place a bed in the lobby as he felt most secure and comfortable there. However, we could not fathom why. It was then that Debashis explained to us that his need to be at a vantage point was crucial so that he could observe the people entering and exiting from the individual rooms on the floor, at least till he fell asleep.

For Noel, music was a fail-safe calming mechanism. Even in the throes of the most severe meltdown, if someone started to sing, he would join in. He always sang beautifully, holding onto the essence of the tune. This book will help parents to search for these sparks of interest in their children, nurture them and take them beyond obsessive interests that isolate children. Parents and educators must strategically use these interests to build self-management skills that will allow neurodivergent children to make friends, as Noel did through his love for singing and music.

Noel leaving was a shock and not a single day goes by when he is not remembered at Shaurya. The biggest lesson he taught all of us was that if something does not work out, there is always going to be a 'next time'!

This book is sure to lift you and make you appreciate life with all its mysteries and challenges.

Rubina Mohan,
Director,
Shaurya Foundation Trust,
New Delhi

Introduction

The challenges a congenitally disabled person faces are usually lifelong. In times of sustainability goals and widespread discourse about equity and inclusion, I think it's important that we start reading and talking more about these challenges. The general awareness and understanding most people have for such a person is pitiably low and unfortunately marked by a noticeable lack of empathy.

I am using the term 'neurologically divergent' to include a wide range of various intellectual, bio-neurological and related physical differences that affect a child's development and progress in routine life.

From the moment the child is clinically diagnosed, barbs are often hurled at both the child and the parents by strangers and even family members and friends out of sheer ignorance, deep-set societal taboos and most worryingly, *fear*.

Yes! A fear of persons with disabilities is often associated with unpredictable behaviours and sometimes even with hostility. It sets up an atmosphere that makes the parents suffer from a sense of guilt, resentment and forced isolation. The reasons for such negative notions typically come from a cage of prejudices, superstitions and incorrect assumptions that have no scientific basis. This invariably engenders discrimination.

When I enquire about the well-being of my childhood friend's neurologically and physically disabled thirty-four-year-old son, the father breaks down and says, with deep anguish and surrender, 'Oh, it's my fate and I have to live with it!' This is a common response and is quite heartbreaking. And it is also how parents get socially conditioned to view the situation, as one of misfortune and despair all the way!

We begin to consider the child 'ashubh'. Inauspicious. An embodiment of bad karma; a mark of stigma. We often feel impelled to hide the child. Even looking at the child fondly is strictly rationed as compared to a neurotypical child.

Dr Yuval Noah Harari, the very popular author, historian and thinker, whom I so admire, cautions, 'It is a great wisdom to accept reality as it is, even if it contradicts most stories that many people believe.'

This has always resonated within me as the father of a non-neurotypical child.

In the realm of neurological disabilities, the negative stories or collective beliefs are what have become entrenched in our society. They ceaselessly produce invisible stumbling blocks for the neurodivergent child as they begin to navigate their developmental path. And needless to say, such negativity demoralises parents deeply, along with the rest of the family, while also gravely compromising the child's progress and adding to their anxieties.

There has been exponential growth in the subject knowledge of neurodiversity owing to advances in research, advances in medicinal therapies, learning devices, educational tools, incredibly easy-to-use teaching apps, access to limitless resources because of the internet boom and many other emergent technologies that have made parents, educators and individuals with autism better equipped with knowledge and tools.

But expert advice, new knowledge of therapies and prescriptions are not the only things that parents need.

They need courage every step of the way, to hold up against societal negativities.

They need the strength to crawl out from the caverns of hopelessness.

They need help to laser cut through the bars of the cage of prejudices.

They need new energy to think differently so as to benefit their child.

They need a growing awareness and understanding that is supportive.

They need emotional support and direction.

They need hope.

So, parents have to hear from other parents facing similar challenges. They have to know they are not alone. They have to know what other parents are going through. They have to learn copiously from other parents' experiences, insights, fears, mistakes, struggles and victories.

Dr Winnie Dunn, Distinguished Professor of Occupational Therapy at the University of Missouri, USA and the recipient of many accolades for her significant contributions to knowledge development in this field, notes in the foreword of *Asperger Syndrome and Sensory Issues* (AAPC Publishers, 2000) a point that remains pertinent in this context: 'Imagine all the ways that we might describe the experiences of living across a span of 50 years. In some ways, perspectives become more complex as we become aware of more and more aspects of living. But in other ways, across the length of time, the simplicity and rhythm of living become more apparent. In addition, both of these ways of characterising living would be different from the way in which we would have characterized each of the decades within the 50 years, because the accumulation of knowledge and insight informs us in a unique way from any single experience. When we can move forward and backward in our thinking about phenomena, patterns can emerge that were not evident in our actual experience of them as individual parts.'

Well, those were the reasons that prompted me to write this book!

Younger parents of children with autism must understand how to recalibrate their own ambitions and priorities in life; how to let go of the urge to vicariously achieve their goals through their kids. They need to know that their child may not be able to form emotional and empathetic ties with friends as we do, and therefore, will lean heavily on their parents, siblings or other family members and their teachers to play the role of the proverbial friend, philosopher and guide.

Above all, parents have to stay sane and begin to appreciate their new kind of life. They have to become fountains of strength and unconditional love.

The trauma cycle in early stages, the question of natural acceptance and love arrives first, the searing pain and then the unending frustrations in the neurodiverse/disability arena—much of it brought on by society—follow. The cumulative effect of all of these can crush a lot of the enthusiasm, drain emotional energy, induce mental complexes and, for some, break the resolve of moving forward in their life's path.

Acceptance of the situation is a steep task for the parents. It needs to be worked upon systematically. It calls for a great deal of mental resolve and strength to permanently deviate from the usual trajectory of life. It calls for a questioning attitude, high levels of empathy, a need to rebuild yourself so that your levels of patience grow a thousandfold from when you started out and the mental strength to not lose hope even if nothing is going your way.

Noel, our son, our first child, was diagnosed with autism spectrum disorder at three-and-a-half years of age. The parenting challenges that Pia (Prof. Bishnupriya Dutt) as his mother and I have faced in our journey with him are what I intend to share with the readers.

At the outset, I must categorically state that every autistic person exhibits unique characteristics of the condition. The nature and severity of impairments and strengths differ in each person on the spectrum, in fact, that is why the term 'spectrum' has been introduced in the diagnostic terminology.

I am not a technically qualified person and I have only my experiences with Noel to draw from. However, that journey has exposed me to many spaces and learnings. So, I do speak with considerable confidence and with a depth of understanding that is authentic, empathetic and inventive.

I have found that the autistic appetite for 'structure' may be a useful frame in understanding the condition and this core concept may provide the lens to analyse behaviour, stimulate thinking and frame new perspectives and strategies to help the autistic child or the young person in their overall development.

This book talks about my discovery of sensory integration issues; the intimidating dimensions of 'the social' and communications (not the same thing as language and verbal skills) through my journey with my son.

It's also an expression of ruminations, vignettes and insights drawn from Noel's very short life of twenty-six years that would be of wider interest. It's the sharing of the belief that love can exist, in all its intensity, in pain, humiliation, grief, respect, compassion and companionship. That the flow of love is unstoppable and supremely empowering.

I write for all the parents of kids with disabilities and neurodiverse conditions. I write so that people in larger society who are unaware, understand and accept the lifelong condition of autism as very much a part of human diversity. I also write for parents everywhere who may pick this book up and read it with a broadminded outlook. I am sure that it will benefit every single parent in their crucial role as an understanding parent.

Why do I say so?

All children benefit from being understood by their parents. All children benefit from being constructively engaged in solving problems that concern them. All children benefit from open lines of two-way communication with their parents. Parents play a very important role in shaping their world view. A child's life is not just about academics and play. The values that they will acquire and hold onto as adults develop when they are children. Their optimism or negativity, the nature of relationships they form in adult life, their levels of empathy, how they face adversity in life—all this and more is heavily influenced by their experiences, parental approaches and their attitudes.

There are foundational insights in this book even for parents raising neurotypical kids to reflect on and that may help in shaping their approaches and practices.

I Know I Am Different

Noel was our first child. He was born close to Christmas Day, on 15 December. In my dreams, I saw my son foremost as a spreader of joy; as one who would embody the values of warm celebration, love, kindness and togetherness. So, I named him Noel.

He was simply an adorable toddler with golden curls and a smile that could light up a room. Like all first-time parents, we would often get excited or fretful over each milestone. All the conventional early milestones were on track for our baby, except for a delayed response when he was called by his name and his eyes would waver, making eye contact difficult. At first, Pia and I did not think about it too much. Back then, I was a manager in an advertising agency and Pia had started her career as a professor at the University of Calcutta.

An image from Noel's toddler days that has remained etched in my mind was his unusual self-play of lining up toy cars. He would arrange them carefully; a small blue toy Honda in the front, then a replica of a farm truck; behind that, a beautiful white Mercedes, then a stylish black car that looked somewhat like a GM Optra, followed by a red Ferrari, a water tanker—a long line of about thirty tiny cars.

I used to be spellbound, not just by the flawless assembly that would curve artfully at several places, but by the incredible concentration that Noel displayed while giving shape to his fantasy. An otherwise hyperactive boy, he would sit quietly, surveying the line, absorbing every little detail of every single simulated vehicle for hours, unperturbed by the noise or loud chatter in the living room or even when people called out his name.

When we walked about in the nearby park, he would gather a handful of sand from the leaping pit, gently release it from his tightly formed fists and remark, 'Baba, it's raining, see!'

He would find greater thrill in watching a see-saw from a few metres away rather than riding it. With some patient observation, I figured out that Noel loved to sing *Merry Go 'Round* in accompaniment to the visual of the fulcrum moving in half-rounds, a rhyme that he had picked up on a preschool CD.

With help from my readings on lateral thinking, I inferred that Noel clearly showed some unusual ways of observing things—what we call creative in regular parlance. There wasn't anything really that could have been a cause for worry whatsoever at that stage. He was a beautiful child who had his quirks.

Noel started at one of the well-known Montessori schools

in Kolkata at two-and-a-half years. It devastated him when I dropped him off at school that first day. He cried hopelessly, standing at the entrance veranda of the school, until he was picked up and carried inside the school by a staff member.

Other kids also suffered the proverbial bout of separation anxiety, but almost all of them glided into the school routine after saying goodbye to their parents within the first few days.

Noel cried heartbreakingly for over thirty days!

After about two months, the head of the school called me to observe Noel. An inexplicable fear gripped me. I watched Noel from a classroom window so that I was not visible to him. She said that he was aloof, that there was something odd about him—that he was happy to be on his own. He showed no interest in the kids around him. Noel stayed away from all the kids in class, even during group activities. During his singing class, he sat at a distance from the rest but smiled and clapped along with them. He was never distraught. He took part in everything, but from a distance and never in a group activity that involved standing close to each other or holding hands while singing or playing games.

That is when the alarm bells went off in our minds and hearts. But then we were reasonably sure it was some psychological issue; perhaps a condition of social withdrawal, as a continuing effect of separation anxiety.

He would never harm any child if they came near him. He merely felt uncomfortable and would step away. We interpreted that (naively, in retrospect) as a strong need for personal space.

We visited various paediatricians and child psychologists in

Kolkata but could not get a proper answer or direction. Those days were filled with anxiety and a sense of groping in the dark. Finally, we went to Mumbai to see a renowned neuro-paediatrician. I remember waiting in a hall in the hospital with others and Noel refusing to sit. He was all excited; he threw away his shoes and started to run from one end of the hall to another, chuckling away, creating a soft, melodic percussion with his barefoot padding down the hall. While all the noise and the unexpected behaviour of our child in the waiting room embarrassed us, I was loath to stop him. In the midst of a very tense situation, Noel's sheer joy at that moment was an elixir for me.

The doctor explained that Noel showed some characteristics of classical autism with several Asperger Syndrome traits as well. He was three-and-a-half-years-old. Neither Pia nor I had heard these terms before. We were told that it was a neurobiological, developmental disorder, and a lifelong condition, which often resulted in a number of pervasive handicaps. Noel was a verbal child but would have to be taught how to express himself, as he would encounter difficulties with language learning and his speech was unlikely to be age appropriate.

We were shattered. Our world had turned upside down.

The doctor recommended watching *Rain Man*, a 1988 Oscar-winning film starring Dustin Hoffman, and reading extensively on the subject of autism education techniques.

These suggestions appeared to be standard operating procedures at that time, perhaps still prevalent, but they were lacking in sensitivity or consideration for what parents were going through.

In retrospect, my view is that asking people to watch that film to learn more about autism can be a misleading suggestion for those with low awareness of autism—not every child with the autism condition is a mathematical savant like the protagonist, Raymond, in the movie.

The doctor also recommended that I take a job transfer to USA or UK. However, if we were to decide to stay on in India, we would need to live in Delhi or Mumbai so that we could get Noel at least the basic educational resources he needed as a child with autism, even if they would not be entirely adequate.

I also received valuable counsel at that point from a psychologist friend, Dr Charles Day, based in Iowa, USA. He jumped in to help us upon hearing about Noel's diagnosis. During a call, he walked me through the pros and cons of uprooting ourselves to move to another country and culture. Pia and I evaluated our options calmly and finally decided to remain in India.

That was 1996. There was no internet service and no Google! So, a speedy marshalling of facts and information was nearly impossible. However, we had to learn all we could about autism spectrum disorder. The desire to know and understand more and more became the new engine of my life.

Following Noel's diagnosis and the subsequent turmoil of our mental balance, we gradually settled into accepting the massive challenge of raising Noel and swiftly dismissed all the dreams we'd had of raising a future scientist, doctor or literary genius. Noel was going to be very different. Our life expectations and the whole approach to raising him was going to have to change. We left Kolkata and moved to Delhi.

By the time Noel had turned five, he had attained reasonably good verbal abilities. His emotional attachment to our car was unusually high; whenever there was something wrong with our car or even when it was away for a routine service or repair, he would go through moderate levels of anxiety and repeatedly ask questions such as, 'When will the car come back? Will the car work? Will the suspension become alright?' He never appeared to be satisfied with the answers given.

I remember the first time my car broke down in the middle of a road with Noel sitting in the backseat. 'Baba, we now have to take the car to Dr Wadhwa. He will make it okay,' he said. In Noel's mind, his regular paediatrician, Dr Wadhwa, was the genius who would be able to fix the car the same way that he would fix him!

The classic overarching autism tendency of sweeping generalisations was pervasive. It was sweet and amusing. All of us at home knew how to cope in those early years. It was easy. But thinking about the future used to get me all worked up and I would lose my sleep.

In order to seek a second opinion from a medical specialist, consult a psychotherapist, and understand autism, Pia and I went to London with Noel. We visited the National Autistic Society (NAS) for guidance.

After numerous meetings with specialists, I learnt about the core of Noel's condition. He had a serious pervasive developmental disorder, one that impairs the ability to communicate and impacts the nervous system in puzzling ways. It leads to motor and muscle coordination deficits and causes speech and language learning impairments, accompanied by heightened sensorial and proprioceptive needs. In Noel's case, the ease with which we 'make sense' of the world that is attributable to our sensory systems (tactile, vestibular, visual, auditory and gustatory systems) would not be available. We could alleviate those deficits through various strategies, but there wasn't a clear-cut formula or therapy.

As the years rolled by, Noel began to show all the characteristics of autism in various degrees of severity (please refer to Appendix One for further information—an extract from the NAS website provides a very useful outline of the condition of autism and the key issues faced in everyday life). We dealt with undeniable stress and tension stemming from the daily prevalence of these issues in key developmental years.

For instance, Noel became disruptive, which was a complex obstacle in social spaces and for early learning as well. He would start flapping hands, clapping loudly, shouting out aloud incessantly while covering both ears with his palms. People would say, 'Look, the boy is shouting his lungs out.' Pacifying him and successfully dissipating the high level of his stress was a challenge that demanded extreme levels of patience. There was also incessant chewing on semi-hard objects like toothbrushes, cardboard, leather wallets, shirt sleeves and so on.

Let me pull back and lay out a broader background for sensory issues and repetitive actions displayed by individuals with autism, Asperger's, ADHD and several other neurodivergent conditions.

I mention here some points by Candance Peterson, an occupational therapist and an expert speaker at the ADDitude

ADHD Experts Webinar titled 'What Is Your Child's Sensory Profile? Strategies For Supporting Children with ADHD And SPD'. This webinar was broadcast on 30 March 2022.

Sensory processing is complicated and occurs with all of us. Many of us have an aversion to strong smell, a sensitivity to bright lights, or a reaction to certain clothing textures. These sensitivities are amplified in children with sensory processing disorders, who may be over- or under-responsive to sensory input, seek specific sensations, or struggle to discern sensory information altogether. For these kids, daily functioning and well-being hinge on sensory needs-and our ability to understand and anticipate them.

Sensory processing is the neurology of how we feel. In this process, we receive information through the body's various senses, organise it and use it and make sense of and interact with the world around us.

We all know about the five senses:

- *Sight*
- *Tactile (touch)*
- *Auditory*
- *Gustatory (taste)*
- *Olfactory (smell)*

Sensory integration specialists point toward the three lesser talked about senses:

- *Vestibular: located in the inner ear, this sense allows us to keep our balance and posture.*
- *Proprioception: also known as body awareness, this sense allows us to determine where our body parts are in relation to one another without us having to look at them.*

- *Interoception: The sense of what's going on inside the body from heart rate, hunger, thirst and even emotions.*

As such, sensory processing disorders can impact the brain's ability to receive, organise, or respond to sensory input via any of the eight senses.

Self-stimulating behaviours, or 'stims' as they are called in autism parlance, are triggered neurobiologically and are understood as sensory system imbalances that are difficult to restrain. For example, an incessant and vigorous clapping of hands is referred to as SPO (Sensory Processing Disorders) and manifests in a variety of ways. In many cases, SPO co-occurs with autism. Such acts caused by enhanced sensory needs are only coping mechanisms. They often appear to metamorphose into pleasurable, soothing, comforting actions at the same time. These could also become relieving outlets for deep anguish or frustration, even when not triggered neurobiologically in that moment. This is an area of considerable intricacy in the autism world.

Noel's 'stim' behaviour—the need to shout aloud often—was triggered by various external factors, but he could never talk about them and delineate the reasons. That was the handicap, just so difficult to relate to.

The trigger could be:

a) Not feeling sure what is going to happen next or being scared about what is coming up. For instance, I used to take him out on the terrace at home and he would scream. He would never answer the question, 'Why are you doing this?' However, I soon realised that it was the continuous flight of the birds high above the terrace that caused his fear and distress.

b) Being pushed too hard to do things, i.e., performance pressure.

c) Not being inclined to do something or not feeling up to it.

d) Feeling bored or acutely lonely.

Trial and error led us to accept and cope with the stim behaviours. First and foremost, we had to be respectful and accepting of the behaviour, having understood that it was usually his characteristic coping mechanism. So, it was pointless to feel irritated or display any signs of annoyance. We had to learn to stay unperturbed and ignore people's reactions to any unconventional spurts of his behaviour. We also found that distracting him helped to get back his focus when there was a learning situation available. We had to choose an appropriate activity that could be sustained for a fairly long period. Needless to say, it had to be something he instantly enjoyed doing, such as playing with cars and trains, listening to music, using scissors to cut out pictures of interest from old magazines, or funny sounds or repetitious audio patterns, like a train entering a station. We avoided bribing him with candy at all costs.

It eventually started becoming quite clear to us that Noel derived comfort in 'structured' activities. Thus began my sustained reflection on the notion of structure and autism behaviour and teaching children through the prism of structure. At the root of the need for structures is possibly the reflection of an inner want to instil predictability and control when the individual does not understand the intent of others or is unsure of their surroundings. It's probably driven by the emotional need to be safe and comfortable.

Taking this insight on the embedding of solution structures and deploying it for the purpose of alleviating the 'stim' so that productive learning or social situations are better managed, while giving him control, became the first part of my self-made toolkit. This was my attempt to flip the pacifying process through distraction into a more 'self-regulatory' mechanism. As Noel was familiar with the audio control knob of the car's music system, I told him he should control the volume of his shouting spree by using an imaginary knob that was right in the 'middle of his chest'.

This was, of course, a wild attempt on my part towards finding a solution. Noel surprised me. He became adept at lowering the volume of his shouts by turning the imaginary knob. Similarly, the stim of periodically flapping his hands was modified with the suggestion: 'Put your hands in your pocket for five minutes when you want to flap your hands, you will feel comfortable.' The six-year-old took to it because there was a simple structure and he was in control and this stayed with him until he was well into his twenties.

Often, he would attempt to mimic a rock singer, yelling at the top of his voice with full gusto! We had to learn to distinguish this from the usual stim shouting. However, turning the knob in response to a visual or whisper prompt for volume control worked even for such scenarios!

Seeing the six-year-old boy's difficulties in visually identifying numbers during initial school sessions, I had a brainwave—why not take Noel to a basement garage of a multi-storied building or a shopping mall and get him to read the number plates of the cars parked? The subject of cars was an instant draw and a certain level of engagement was assured.

I began this experimental exercise of number recognition—pointing toward a numeral on a nameplate, I said, 'Noel, read the number.'

Noel responded with focus, 'Seven.' Correct!

I continued, 'Now, what is after seven?'

Noel's answer was eight. I pointed to the next numeral on a license plate—it was a two.

'What comes after seven?'

Noel indicated that it was eight again. A couple of attempts later, the boy's answer remained unchanged. I started the whisper prompt technique to get his close attention.

'Look again, that's a two after the seven.'

Noel answered emphatically, 'Not two, eight!'

It dawned on me that the framing of the question was faulty. Noel replaced the context on hand with the number sequence which he had memorised by rote. To him, no matter the order of numbers on the license plate, eight came after seven, not two! Noel's perceptional mode was not like ours. My question was interpreted literally, and this overshadowed all other stimuli, including the pointing or prompting.

The immediate context was blurred in his mind on hearing a rote trigger: 'What is after?'

In this way, the transposing of words in the language of instruction from one context to an unrelated context posed a problem of perception for Noel all the time.

Another learning rather early on was when I used to ask Noel, 'How do we travel to London?'

'By bus!' he answered confidently.

'No, no, how can we travel by bus—London is very far. You are confused!'

Noel persisted, 'First bus, then plane!'

This was the moment when the penny dropped. The bus takes us from the airport terminal to the tarmac to board the flight. The bit by bus is not forgotten. His memory etched the full structure and sequence of the travel modes. The fact that there would never be a broad overview from Noel became evident.

In the following chapters, I will walk my readers through the importance of structure in Noel's journey of growing up and its myriad effects—some very complicated—and how his ceaseless need for structure could be transformed into out-of-the-box learning opportunities. Beset in the challenge of 'structure' lay also the potential pathways for managing difficult emotions and behaviour, sometimes even fuelling motivation for learning. Yes, there's much to unpack in terms of helpful strategies.

Even in the face of erratic behaviour, one thing that occurred unfailingly in our home was light-hearted teasing, arm-wrestling, cartwheeling for fun, playing hide-and-seek and lots of loud singing (even though Pia and I are no singers, we always played along with the boy's on-demand singing). An overarching atmosphere of goofiness was always the cushion, not only for Noel, but for us as well.

Noel's core strength lay in learning by listening—the audio mode was his life's anchor. He could speak English, Bengali and Hindi, and his skills and comprehension, though not age-appropriate, were his functional strengths.

In terms of receptive and expressive communication, Noel made good progress, year by year. By listening, he easily picked up difficult words in all three languages. His addiction to old songs on YouTube helped expand his vocabulary.

He could understand and appropriately use long and difficult English words such as 'hypochondriac', 'extinguish', 'transparent', 'disappointment', 'disaster', 'reckless', 'comfortable', 'worried', 'surfaces' and phrases like 'push and pull' or 'blank space' (yanked from popular Taylor Swift songs) and so on. It was a similar case with Hindi and Bengali.

He could not read (beyond a small stock of three- to six-lettered commonly used English words) but could readily recognise brand logos, such as McDonald's, Pepsi, Coke, Toyota and Honda. Those which held a brand allure for him were top-of-the-mind, as expected.

He struggled to write. He never went beyond copying words from a card placed in front of him, but he loved to write his name and he did so with much flair! He did it better with a gripper placed around the pencil or pen. That then became his signature.

He learnt the basics of using the keyboard on a computer at school, but his capability for typing out his small stock of English words was limited. While he had verbal capabilities, he was severely handicapped when it came to writing and reading.

However, trial and error helped me understand that Noel could write somewhat better when I provided him support with my stretched right palm to his writing grip. So, seated next to each other, we practised handwriting for hours. This activity was very calming for him. It prevented disruptive behaviour and helped us bond. It became a ritual for us from his sixth year to his twenty-fifth!

We often travelled to Kolkata on vacations. At the New Delhi railway station, I used to watch Noel with interest as we waited for the Rajdhani Express. He would look in the direction of the track, waiting for the train to make its appearance, anticipation written on his face.

When asked, 'Why is Kolkata your favourite city, Noel?', he would respond cheerfully, 'Because I love my grandmothers, Didaan and Thamma, my grandfathers, Utpal Dadu and Dada Bhai, Boro Pishi and Ranjit Da, (my elder sister, Mitali, and brother-in-law), Kookie Jar (a bakery), Mocambo (a restaurant), Balaram Mullick (a Bengali sweet and desserts shop), Bhojo Hari Manna (an authentic Bengali restaurant), Tolly Club and Dadu's library.'

Every day he would want to talk about Kolkata!

Our daughter, Ahvana, Noel's Bonu, (an affectionate way of addressing his sister), was then a year old and she grew up to be a wonderful bossy little sister who was deeply attached to and protective of Noel. Even so, they had their usual sibling rivalries in those years growing up—squabbling over belongings and space; the harmless jostle for attention and fighting over the relative share of importance.

Whenever Noel found Ahvana having a long, excited conversation with her mother or with me after an outing or a day at school, he would without fail interject, with mild irritation, 'Bonu, don't say the same thing again and again.' This was an oft-used taunt to tick off his sister. It was possibly rooted in his feeling of being sidelined in a particular situation for too long. He wanted some of the attention of the people around—more so if it was his mum or dad!

These, I counted as moments of triumph in the social space. They did not conform to the typical understanding of day-to-day successes. Yet, I would mark them as a step forward on planet autism.

Flash forward to early youth: once, a little irked by her nineteen-year-old brother's constant jabber, my daughter, then fifteen, asked, 'Hey, do you know how old you are?' in a brutal sisterly taunt.

Noel swiftly retorted, 'I am independent!'

His thought, as far as I could read, was, if the apex attribute is being independent, then age simply pales into insignificance.

By the time he reached seventeen, he had overturned the common autistic traits of self-isolation—being uncomfortable with the physical presence of people around him. He was no more caught up with obsessive narrow interests. He had figured out how to deal with things and situations that caused stress and anxiety. On being nudged, he could restrain his stim in a public space. With my repeated mentions, Noel had grasped the concept of public space in outward behaviour.

It was after much inner conflict that I had resolved to tell him why those prompts were necessary. Taking him aside, I would say, 'Noel, you are lovable. You are different from me and many others, so I need to remind you about public spaces.' His clear and empathic response always was along the lines of, 'I have autism, Baba, I know' and 'I will always be a gentleman in public.' Those prompts from me in public zones were always with the same volume and tone. Thus, a structured solution was invented and, over time, got wired into Noel's routine. He became conscious of the public and would apply himself to the best of his abilities.

Noel became a very interesting man to be around as he crossed twenty. He was confident, secure, kind, affectionate, empathetic and had genuine warmth for the people around him. He trusted them and believed in their goodness. He never withdrew or distanced himself from others. He wanted to reach out to others but struggled with the means of doing so. That struggle was ever present, but that did not frustrate him beyond reasonable levels.

I believe this was because of our consistent approach of giving him his personal space, letting him lead, encouraging him to teach us how to align with him, communicating with him gently while completely respecting his differences and, most of the time, enjoying them.

The cracking of structure-led solutions and the all-around

adjustments were never easy. Though I strove valiantly to push back the frequent wave of despair ('Why us?') by the sound rationale of a dictum ('It is not targeted at us and it really isn't something that can destroy us'), I have to admit that the downers, many a time, were too forceful and the rush of despair very palpable.

The sooner that parents come to grips with the 'you are not targeted' aspect of their self-dialogue, the better it is for their sanity and self-confidence. It is also better for the team spirit within the family unit. As for neurotypical children, the importance of early childhood cannot be overemphasised; it determines their core sense of security and helps shape their social dimension. Psychologists always say that home is the seat of learning. Attitudes towards others take shape here, surprisingly early in life. The relations and experiences with members of the family sets a foundation for attitude formation. The fundamentals of this phenomenon do not change in the raising of children with a disability.

Trusting your spouse and close family members along with openly communicating the hardships and challenges is healthy and helpful. It keeps your energy up. This, admittedly, is easy to say and often difficult to accomplish. The reason I say this is to urge my readers to recognise that this force can be leveraged within the family unit and that this eventually helps everyone. This is the force to latch onto forever. Sharing everyday struggles with each other helps normalise them. This takes some time, but does yield positive results.

Being able to separate your ego from other people's

perceptions of your neurodivergent child provides a buffer against the jabs from the world around you. Sometimes, they come from people who are supposed to be close to the subject: expert counsellors meant to provide professional direction and help, child psychologists, doctors, educators and even close family members.

The neurodivergent mind comes with all the vulnerabilities of a neurotypical mind amplified many times over. Raising a child is hard enough, let alone one with a disability. Just as nobody is specifically trained to become a parent, nobody is specifically trained to become the parent of a child with a disability either. The path is full of challenges and no generalised method can help in the development of the child. The trial-and-error approach is then the norm to be followed.

Another perspective I wish to add (in the sphere of parenting a child with autism): just when you think your strenuous efforts have been wasted, the proverbial miracle strikes.

We have to allow the child to find their own path of seeing, feeling and perceiving the world through a lens that is extraordinary. Miracles often come out of that alignment, filling us invariably with the thrill of victory, laughter, beautiful sentiments and treasured moments of fun.

In parallel, one has to build up tons of resilience and openness and slog towards a joyful attitude of acceptance. Let the child lead the path as we walk by their side and aid their process of discovery and learning.

I have always reflected on the premise: should we not place our line of vision to go beyond acceptance? Why not find the hidden talents and nurture them gently and patiently without setting big expectations? Let the child succeed in small steps. Let the child feel secure and happy in their accomplishments. Look for small wins so that you can take the stumble in your stride. Celebrate the minor successes and block any form of comparison with other children. The child should be shielded from an implicit consciousness of being less.

It is for the parents to first accomplish a whole-hearted acceptance and then achieve the freedom to glide beyond the bounds of acceptance by reinventing themselves.

————

I was at a pathology lab for a blood test and Noel was with me as part of my always-on teaching-moments strategy, which involved exposing him to a new situation and then explaining what it was all about in slow, simple sentences for him to learn something new. When the lab assistant was closing in on me with his intimidating needle, Noel suddenly grabbed his hand: 'Don't take Baba's blood, take mine for Baba's test.' Noel could not bear to see me in pain! Emotions set ablaze! A dramatic turn! I had not given a good explanation of why it had to be my blood and why his blood could not be a substitute. My goof-up.

————

It was 22 April, Lenin's birth anniversary.

Noel was twenty-one years old then, and he was glowing with excitement. He was full of anticipation as we drove to Nehru Park for Lenin's birth anniversary celebrations. It has the largest expanse of green that I have seen in Delhi. To attend a 'birthday party' in such serene outdoors was sheer delight for the young man.

However, on arrival, he was visibly disappointed.

'Has Lenin arrived? It is his birthday! Has he forgotten? Call me when he is here!' Noel declared and stomped away from the crowd that had gathered. I saw him sulk and seat himself away from the gathering on a park bench.

What a blooper this was! It had entirely escaped us that a proper context had to be set for Noel. We forgot to tell him that Lenin was no more and that birthday celebrations can happen even after a person is dead!

––––––

On the usual morning-question drill with my son to nudge his thinking: 'Which is the one activity that you like most?'

I expected him to say something along the lines of eating pizza or ice cream, playing tennis or golf, cycling in the forest, meeting people he likes or listening to his music playlist.

Noel thought for a while and answered, 'Coming back home!'

CHAPTER TWO

My Blue Corsa

Whenever I got back from the office, Noel would be thrilled. He would sparkle with joy at seeing me step into the house. This reaction was the same for his mum and had been so since he was a small boy.

Watching him in that euphoric state naturally filled me with happiness, regardless of how my day had been. Any negative thoughts that may have clouded my mind would be washed away instantly.

However, if I stepped in earlier than I normally did from work, contrary to expectations, the reaction would be quite the opposite. To my utter astonishment, Noel would run amok in the opposite direction.

What we realised then was that Noel viewed my returning home at an earlier time to be an abrupt change in the set 'structure' and he had difficulty dealing with it. The routine that he was used to was being disrupted. Instead of his usual wide smile, he would yell in perplexed agony. His behaviour suggested: 'Why did you come back so much before your stipulated time!? Now you have disturbed me and I find it hard to cope with this unannounced change.'

The bizarre issue of how 'sudden transitioning' to a new scenario could make him so distraught was a new discovery. Noel was so different. It's natural to jump from one scenario to another, one physical environment to another for us—we barely pause to transition or reset our minds. The mind automatically opens a to-do list as you enter the marketplace after office, or walk into a pub after a game of badminton. We go through dozens of transitions in a day, but we stay goal-oriented in every set-up. This was not obviously the case with Noel. He needed time to prepare his mind before entering a new scene. I am guessing the overwhelming effect of unfamiliar sights, voices, people and the colours of his surroundings had to be processed by pushing out what had come before, somewhat like closing all the files on your laptop before opening a new set of files for the next task. That takes time.

The idea of giving him time before a transition and not hurrying him became important. And further, it became standard to arm him with a simple structure to manage the transition. In this case, the structure that I tried arming him with was a verbal cue, spoken in an affirmative tone: 'Now, wait for five minutes!' I used this cue whenever he was to enter a new set of surroundings. The wait, even if not for precisely five minutes, appeared to help him a lot. To him, it was a reassuring indicator that he could take his time before proceeding to the new area. I first used it when he was to be dropped to school. The car-to-classroom transition strategy worked and then it became a permanent fixture in our lives. The same strategy was used when he moved to vocational education after his school years and then at workplaces.

However, since Noel was going to a mainstream school which had special education, the noise, the confusion, the loud sound of shoes hitting the ground as children ran wildly into the building during the morning rush hour—all of it caused a huge derailment in Noel's mind. To always offer him a calm transition was challenging.

So, in addition to the five-minute trick, I began dropping him off at school half an hour after school started, when the early morning rush had subsided. This worked! This allowed him to transition into the school environment. The school authorities made this late arrival an allowance and for that, I was thankful.

As discussed earlier, many children on the autism spectrum have the all-pervasive need for a structure of occurrences (let's call them definitive patterns). They find solace in consistency and predictability. This characteristic need for 'rigidities' appeared complex and one never knew in what ways this may manifest in everyday life. The shifts from one set-up to another, from one structure to another require a careful understanding of the child's needs. This entails close observation, patience and analytical thinking.

When Noel turned seven, in order to indulge his narrow interest in cars (a delineated feature of autism; please refer to Appendix One), I started taking him to various car showrooms on Sundays and this became our Sunday ritual for almost ten years! I would take him to see the arrival of new car models on Mathura Road in New Delhi. We would move from a Toyota to a Chevrolet and then to a Hyundai showroom and we would check out the repair/service garages that were adjacent to the showrooms. On reaching the car showroom, Noel would be ecstatic. Letting out squeals of excitement, he would hop into the showroom exclaiming aloud the brand name: 'This is Chevrolet!' or 'Now we have come to Toyota!'

This activity provided us with small windows of opportunity to teach Noel about communication and other vital things; the idea was to get the boy at his most receptive mode for new learnings. The notion that early intervention/teaching should be confined to the schoolroom or restricted to the home had to be discarded. Noel was ten when I taught him to go to the sales attendant and ask if he could pick up a couple of promotional leaflets. A classic social situation riddled with difficulties. The prospect of a self-initiated interchange of any kind was a challenge. Soon, he learnt to strike up a conversation meaningfully with the sales attendant. On one occasion, a showroom salesperson told him they had run out of brochures and a reprint was underway. Noel enquired voluntarily, 'Printing at Thompson Press?'

Noel had gone on a school trip several years ago to observe how printing was done at the well-known Thompson Printing Press in Faridabad. He'd thought there was only one printing press in the world! I was very surprised and excited to see him remember the name of the press and the takeaway from that school trip suddenly after so many years.

At the end of his car showroom rounds, he would promptly place the leaflets and brochures into a plastic folder bearing his name on the cover and clasp the folder under his arm like a prized possession.

One Sunday, while driving back from the showroom ritual with Noel (then ten) and Ahvana (then six), I missed the turn to get onto the usual road towards home and was forced to take a longer one. The change in the route got Noel terribly riled up. I realised I was in the middle of an experience that I had only read about in books on autism. I was stupefied; it was actually happening before my eyes.

Noel started crying. His tantrum was about to erupt, I could sense that. Ahvana tried to pacify him, saying, 'As long as we reach home, how does it matter, Noel?' But he kept crying. We got rather irritated with his silly outburst and decided to ignore him.

We got home. Noel was still very upset and crying intermittently. I ended the approach of ignoring him and tried to assuage him by categorically promising that the next time we went, we would stick to the regular route on our return. However, he continued to be disconsolate.

Noel refused to have dinner and was absolutely miserable. Yet, he would not tell us why he was so upset. I began to get frustrated. There was only one thing to do—drive back to the showroom and follow the normal route to get home. I resolved to not miss the bloody turn this time!

Noel gradually calmed down in the car as we settled in yet again for the drive. When we reached the showroom, Ahvana pointed to it. We took the usual U-turn to return home. Order returned instantly to Noel's world, he was calm and all was okay.

The myriad manifestations of this phenomenon became an obsession for me, if only to find strategies to manage them to Noel's advantage. Noel was happiest when he was being taught numerals and counting using toy vehicles and then walking into shopping mall parking lots to practice counting. Replacing the standard addition/subtraction textbook teaching at school, thus bringing alive the 'structure' of counting by actual cars all around him.

Noel was drawn to cars very early in life. In fact, any mode of transportation (aeroplanes, trains, motorboats) was a very exciting subject for him. He was entranced by them visually and by their characteristic sounds. Between the ages of eight and ten, Noel had developed an emotional attachment of an altogether new dimension to a new car provided to me by my employer.

The car was a Prussian blue Corsa from GM. This one was very special and Noel called it 'Blue Corsa'. He absolutely adored the gleaming Chevrolet sedan. It was nicely rounded on all sides and was quite different from the sharp, macho and intimidating look that was in vogue in those days. I always thought that the reason for Noel's absolute attraction to the car was because it resembled one of his toy cars from when he was a toddler. It was identical in colour and possessed that characteristic rounded look. I asked Noel about why he had been so drawn to the Corsa many times over the years. He never answered. Maybe the feeling was too abstract for him to describe. However, when

I resorted to my MCQ style of questioning where I would give him three options, he would respond affirmatively to the toy car resemblance option. My presumption on this one proved to be accurate.

He would travel to school in the Blue Corsa and loved going out in it. The car was with us for two years. But then a time came when I had to give it up for a swankier car, a Toyota Altis, following my promotion at the company. When this finally happened, I did not spend too much time thinking about how to prepare Noel for the impending exit of the Blue Corsa from his life.

That was a massive mistake in hindsight. The leasing company executive arrived one morning and it was goodbye to Blue Corsa. What followed shattered us. There was an outburst every morning that would last for two to three hours and his temper tantrums would be non-stop. Noel would cry continuously and throw things around to register his protest (he intuitively chose non-breakable stuff, fortunately).

Sometimes, on Sundays when we were all home and he had a captive audience, his crying and whining for the Blue Corsa would go on for rest of the day! This is not an exaggeration; he would actually sob till night-time. It had devastated Noel! For us, it was mentally debilitating watching him cry the whole time. He was a tortured soul who could not focus on anything. We tried everything that common sense prompted us to do, but nothing worked. It had been twenty-five days already and the magnitude of the trauma would just not subside.

Finally, I consulted a child psychiatrist. For the Indian parent, it is not typical to think of a professional psychologist or a psychiatrist for remedial advice. There was much dilly-dallying, I have to admit, on our end. The doctor explained to Pia and me that the situation was exactly the same as that of losing a pet. As Noel had difficulties in processing certain occurrences, the sudden surfacing of unpredictable events was much harder for him. The emotional loss refused to recede. Then it also dawned on me that the phenomenon of anthropomorphism, i.e., the attribution of human-like qualities, behaviour, characteristics to an object or animal as is done in the world of children's storytelling, cartoons and so on could also be a reasonable supportive explanation. For Noel, the Corsa was human-like.

The psychiatrist advised us to put Noel on Risperidone tablets that would help calm him down and allow him to return gradually to his regular schedule. He also advised me to take Noel to the place where he could see the Corsa and spend a little time with the car.

My finance manager from the office helped me locate the car leasing company's garage and voila! I spotted the Blue Corsa in a gigantic parking complex. It swept away Noel in an emotional rush.

He saw it in the midst of dozens of cars lined up, pointed at it with a gleam in his eyes and ran towards the car, calling out, 'My Blue Corsa! My Blue Corsa!' He gently placed his fingers on the car bonnet and said aloud, 'I miss you, Blue Corsa,' in a tone that has remained etched in my mind since then. He kissed the bonnet, the doors, the headlights and then said goodbye to his Blue Corsa as I stood a few metres away, clicking pictures. It was gauche, one may say, but it tugged at my heart. It was like the climax of a love story unfolding. It really felt like that!

I came to realise that Noel had an enormous capacity to love something. Even though it may be described as a clinically rigid and obsessive attachment, a characteristic of the autism spectrum (the analogy used by the psychiatrist was remarkably precise), the Corsa was Noel's lifeline, his great love, his dear pet.

On my return to the office the next day, I walked straight into my finance manager's office, first, to thank him for arranging the visit to the leasing company's garage and then to enquire, in all earnestness, whether I could buy the old Corsa from the car leasing company. He saw the absolute helplessness, the despair in a father's eyes and pleaded with me not to do so as it would be an unwise financial decision.

Clearly, Noel could form deep emotional bonds of great intensity. The question that kept bobbing in my head was just how could I give him a handle beyond the calming drugs he'd been prescribed to enable him to cope with the situation? The apprehension that the prolonged use of drugs would have some side effects unknown to us—admittedly not scientific thinking on my part—has always stayed with me.

I realised that apart from his genuine emotional bonding, there was a compelling need for the Corsa-related structure to persist. So, the solution to a ruptured structure could be a replacement structure. I thought of introducing the concept of something becoming old and therefore unable to perform.

I said, 'Noel, like a daddu (grandfather), your Blue Corsa has become old and cannot perform, or even accelerate anymore, so we had to send him to rest. We must accept that. That's the reason we need a new car. Of course, we will always remember and love Blue Corsa.' I chose my words carefully, using a gentle tone.

Noel repeated every word like a chant, in exactly the same tone. As I heard him echo my words, I could not hold my tears back. I went on in this vein like a parrot whenever Noel broke down over his beloved Blue Corsa. The words 'cannot perform' and 'cannot accelerate' were new to his vocabulary, but with repeated mentions, he understood what they meant and could make the connection.

He would repeat exactly what I said several times. It was echolalia, but he understood as well. It calmed him down. It became the 'reason-why' and, eventually, a new thought structure—a surrogate structure—took root.

The prescribed drug, Risperidone, also continued. The situation improved. It took one entire year for his meltdowns to recede. In the initial days, I found him kicking the Toyota car whenever he came out of the car. His distaste for the new creature was evident!

I remained on tenterhooks even while I was sitting in long-drawn high-level business meetings, fearful of a phone call from the school administration with a stern message, 'Noel is having an emotional outburst, can you please pick him up from school right away.'

However, with the passage of time, Noel came around to accepting and, gradually, even liking the new car. I considered this transition to a new surrogate structure, although gradual, to have been accomplished with a consistent strategy of careful articulation, clarity and simplicity. Over time, he appeared to reconcile to bigger changes as well in life in general and accepted that they were inevitable. If I could paraphrase his thoughts: Noel understood that these are sad episodes and a painful part of life, but things that one just had to cope with.

When Noel turned twenty, I gifted him poster-sized colour prints of the photographs I'd clicked of him standing with his Blue Corsa at the leasing company garage. He was thrilled. He placed them in his personal folder in his bedroom cupboard with his collection of all other pictures of things that he liked to talk about—just pleasant, vivid memories layered with a healthy dose of nostalgia. Even at twenty-five, he would still recall in a pensive way, at least once a week, his Blue Corsa with amazing loyalty and love. Looking at him making that moving reconciliation with his 'lost love' filled my heart with adulation for the boy.

There appeared to be a life message in his resolve. 'My Blue Corsa is old. He is beautiful. He has become a daddu but he has not gone to heaven yet. He is still there, resting in that garage. He can perform a little bit. He can accelerate a little bit. You can still drive him a little bit. You can enjoy little bit.'

The phenomenon of structure in play in Noel's behaviour and thoughts always bewildered us. Here is another little story that throws more light on new angles concerning the complexity of strands within a structure. At fourteen, Noel would sing, often in full throttle, the songs on the playlists of his five favourite CDs. He would load the CDs into the car's music system each time he got into the car. Noel never exercised the option of replacing those five CDs with any other. He was locked into the structure of listening to only those very CDs in the car.

The listening ritual would always start with the carol:

The first Noel, the angels did say
Was in fields where they lay keeping their sheep
On a cold winter's night that was so deep
Noel, Noel, Noel, Noel
Born is the king of Israel
They looked up and saw a star
Noel, Noel, Noel, Noel

This was his number one favourite, as his name was a part of the song. It made him feel important. It was a treat to watch him sing along to every song that played on those CDs. He would lay back in the front seat, supremely relaxed, with the seat reclined for maximum comfort. While travelling in the car with Noel, there was no option of listening to any other music of your choice. He was the boss in this department and he called the shots on what music would play in the car. He was indeed the self-appointed car DJ!

We followed his explicit rules of listening to his music in the car for almost three years and, like Noel, everyone who travelled in the car with him had to be fixated on the same songs. While leaving the car to go back to our apartment from the garage, the CDs were always with him. He would clutch onto them like a toddler holding onto his teddy bear. The unchanging structure soothed his nerves and provided him with an affirmation of his possessions.

There was once such a hullabaloo at home because Noel could not find his CDs. All hell broke loose. Noel had gone to the bathroom and as soon as he came out, we heard a shrill scream.

'Where are my CDs?'

'Who has taken them!'

'This is horrible!'

'I am frustrated.'

'I am angry.'

'A thief has stolen my CDs!'

'Call the police, now!'

Pia walked into the room. 'What has happened, Noel? Why can't you keep your things carefully?' A full-fledged search operation began. Everybody at home stopped whatever they were doing and jumped in to look for the CDs as Noel continued screaming his head off. It was a scene straight out of a comedy show with our cook, driver, maid, Ahvana, Pia and I in frantic search of the missing set of CDs. Once they were found, there was a collective sigh of relief. Noel was quiet again. Life was back to normal.

By the way, those CDs could not be played inside the house. That was also a rule that we had to conform to. The structure allowed them to be played only in the car. Once, I tried pushing the issue and said 'Noel, today is a rainy day, as we are not going out. Let's listen to the music on my laptop.' Noel was agitated. 'No, no, never!' he exclaimed vehemently. His resistance was so puzzling. 'I thought you love these CDs, let's play them and enjoy your favourite songs. Relax with Baba, come on.' He just walked away quietly. It meant the CDs were to be only played in the car. No flexibility, no exceptions and no lure of any sort of gratification could bend the rules of this structure.

Then, the day arrived when I had to give up the car for a new one. The thought of the impending trauma and the excruciating pain he might go through petrified me. But I had learnt my lesson with the saga of the Blue Corsa. This time, I started talking to him about the change of car a month in advance. I took him to various car showrooms to show him options for other cars, thus drawing him into choosing our new car. Eventually, he shortlisted three cars to decide from and I made sure that the one my employer would provide me was on that shortlist. This also meant that, over and over again, Noel had to be taken to those three car showrooms to look up the cars in consideration and pick up the sales pamphlets for each car.

Things were under better control this time with regard to the impending change of car. Call it a pre-sell if you wish! On the day I had to send away the Toyota Altis, I asked Noel to come along for a drive, a farewell drive. Noel seemed sad that day. He had grown to like this car, but it was nowhere close to the intensity of his first love, the Blue Corsa.

Noel got in for his last drive in the Toyota Altis. He came in with his CDs in tow. He inserted them into the player. 'Baba, I love this music. I love my CDs,' he said. When we got back from the drive, Noel was pensive. He stepped out of the car and sauntered towards the lift in deep thought. I suddenly spotted the discs inside the player. He had left them intact in the music player.

That was so unexpected, I called out with much urgency, 'Noel, your CDs are still in the car! This car will be taken away by the leasing company. Please take them out!' Noel half-turned, stood still for a moment looking at me and then just walked away without the CDs.

Moments later, as I parked and switched off the engine, the penny dropped. Noel's pleasure of listening to the CDs was associated with this particular car and this music system. All the 'happy' objects linked to this car should also exit from his life with the car. They were interlocked in this structure. The evenness of a structure must be maintained in his mind and we had to respect it.

The rigidity of structure can become an impediment in the way of learning new things. It appeared to be an impenetrable wall. The natural fluidity of tackling everyday situations that one is used to was not something you could ever take for granted.

Once, at an upscale café, Noel and I were out for a Sunday afternoon treat. Sandwiches were among the big highs for Noel, ever since we had ended six years of his GF/CF (gluten-free/casein-free) diet plan.

While Noel was on the GF/CF diet, he would always pick up the McDonald's tray with burgers, settle into his seat, remove both the burger buns, place them on the side of the tray and bite into the burger patty. The structure was automated and he never bit into the bread with gluten. One wondered if he would ever show any interest in bread or anything that tastes and looks like bread ever again. Diet regulation and management in the autism spectrum is a vast expert topic and I shall not delve into that here. But then I have to briefly outline one of the central issues that is much researched: the leaky gut syndrome which constitutes the context of the widely known GF/CF diet remedy. The leaky gut syndrome is a condition where the natural intestinal barriers are damaged and this may allow permeation of toxic substances into the bloodstream, leading to derailment of the neurological system and may cause a host of health consequences. The GF/CF eating plan avoids foods that contain gluten (found in many breads and cereals) and casein (found in milk products) that may generate toxins that are harmful. Noel was medically advised to follow a GF/CF diet plan. We diligently followed it for six successive years. However, after the six-year ban, bread was gradually brought back into his diet. We had taken a conscious decision to slowly phase out the GF/CF diet as his hyperactivity had come down (though medically, the advice was to continue the diet strategy). When the diet regimen was eased out slowly, he began to show an uncontrollable craving for bread.

At the café that day, as he polished off the giant triangles of bread with the layers of mayonnaise and roasted vegetables, I mentioned softly that he should always be a gentleman and remember to do the right thing after he finished eating. Never letting a teachable moment go by idly had become a persistent mantra for me! An innate quirk that I had developed that seemed irrepressible.

He was not always receptive to these teaching moments. But this time, Noel responded with considerable elegance; he used the paper napkin flawlessly and placed the cutlery in the right fashion on the plate, displaying gentlemanly etiquette. Soon, it was time to leave. I was at the door and I half-turned to check if he was following me. Instead, Noel was still in there and sauntering around with the ceramic plate in his hands. Two cups, saucers and spoons were stacked on the plate and balanced precariously. I figured out that our young 'gentleman' was looking for the trash bin so he could throw it all away!

I had taught him to dispose of the plastic trays and cardboard boxes that accompany a fast-food meal into the bins placed inside outlets such as McDonald's. He had erroneously inferred that every meal was meant to conclude by throwing the crockery and cutlery into the bin!

I missed a heartbeat. I could hear in my head the impending crash of broken ceramic cups and plates and yelled from the door, 'This is not McDonald's!' It worked. Noel stopped in his tracks. A waiter also heard me and rushed to help Noel.

Noel gave me a priceless look—one that said that it was Baba's fault, as it was I who had asked him to do the gentlemanly thing and he had only been complying. His generalisations were awkward but always came from a line of logic that we could not catch instantly. The logic here was that the overall look and feel of the place were akin to a McDonald's so the disposal of used plates and cutlery must be the same. It certainly rankled him why generalisations in social situations did not always work.

———

'Will you take me to the Ferrari showroom on Mathura Road? Can we go tomorrow?'

I was a bit surprised by Noel's question. He has never been there and had just passed by once, a few months back. A spontaneous sermon from me on how we should not crave expensive material things in life followed.

A quick reply in a plain tone from Noel: 'Baba, I only want to pick up a Ferrari brochure from that showroom.'

———

In 2019, after leading a somewhat extravagant lifestyle in Delhi, and having increasing concerns about the future, I was furthering the agenda to downscale and cut back on unnecessary expenses, a new, cool, pragmatic way that I had been preaching to my friends and family members to adopt. An unexpected thing happened. In my absence, our driver, Dev Kumar, who had been with us for twenty years, started answering Noel's repeated question, 'Which car will my Baba buy after this car becomes old?' with a sarcastic jibe, 'Arey, tera Baba auto kharidey ga ... samjha?! Three-wheeler auto! (Your dad will buy a three-wheeler auto, you understand?)'

Noel, unable to grasp the wicked sarcasm, became very concerned. He was worried about how an auto could seat all the family members. The ludicrousness of an auto becoming a family vehicle and any consciousness about social or income status association did not appear to bother him. His counter to the jibe was earnest, 'Dev bhaiya, Baba does not know how to drive an auto, so he will never buy one.'

When my driver narrated this to me, I could not stop laughing.

CHAPTER THREE

One More Day in Rome?

The years seemed to zip past so fast. Noel turned eleven. By then, his method that resolved the ruptures in a deep-set structure was a silver lining that had taken form over the years.

We were on a family vacation in Rome, staying at a quaint place called the Tirreno Hotel, about four kilometres from the railway station. From Noel's point of view, the first highlight of our stay was the separate room that he had to himself, which had a door opening to our room. The second was the sumptuous buffet breakfast at the hotel.

Noel revelled in all the attention that was showered on him by the Italians. At one of the pizza restaurants near the Trevi fountain, Noel, the charmer and the foodie, was told that as soon as he finishes school, he would have a job in the restaurant as a kitchen assistant, simply because all the staff members loved the boy's happy face. His presence would cheer everyone up.

I remember muttering to Pia, 'So there is one place on

earth where Noel will always get a job. That is reassuring, what say?' We had a good laugh as we were perennially in a state of anxiety when it came to his future. Would he ever get a job to sustain himself as an adult?

The fabled Italian affinity for children and their spontaneity were evident wherever we went. After five wonderful days, the time had come to leave the warmth and hospitality of Rome behind. Noel was crestfallen, as he always was when a holiday or visit, to a place he had just begun to like, came to an end. In his usual way, he tried to negotiate, 'Just one more day, Baba? I love Rome.' It was his constant refrain, even as we arrived at the airport for departure to board a midday Ryanair flight to London, our next destination.

However, as he settled into his seat on the aeroplane, his mood changed. 'I am going to be flying in the sky,' he exclaimed with glee as the flight took off. He followed this with the Bengali version, '*Ami, ami aakashey oorchie, ami oorchie, ami oorchie!*'

After the thrill of taking off, Noel was looking forward to an unhurried enjoyment of the warm, delicious food that would be served by a smiling flight attendant. His eyes gleamed with anticipation. However, in our hurry, we had missed out on an important act that many parents of ASD children miss out on rather often—the preparation for what is coming up, especially if there is any deviation expected from a familiar structure that is already encoded in the child's mind.

You may ask—what in this humdrum setting of an aeroplane cabin could prove to deviate from a fixed, predictable structure? Noel asked me with a note of impatience in his voice, 'Baba, when will they serve lunch?' I answered absent-mindedly, 'I am not sure.' I did not realise then that Pia and I had made a big blunder. Ryanair is a low-cost airline and they do not serve food on-board. Noel was flying a low-cost airline for the first time. In India, he had been on flights, but that was before the arrival of the new aviation chapter of no-meals, no-frills airlines.

So, he had not been told that this flight was going to be different and that food would not be served. Not prepared for this predicament, I could now feel his anticipation escalating. He was muttering repeatedly under his breath in his characteristic self-talk, 'Ryanair air hostess will serve me exciting lunch soon!'

Finally, the air hostess arrived. She smiled and handed a small bottle of water to Noel. He smiled back at her. Then he asked earnestly, 'When will you serve me lunch on a tray?' The air hostess, who spoke broken English, replied curtly, 'No food. Only water!'

That crisp reply remained etched in Noel's mind for twenty years. He recounted that phrase whenever there was talk of any impending air travel. He would check, again and again, whether it would be a case of 'Only water!' or if there would be food on the flight as well.

So, Noel's first encounter with a no-meals, no-frills airline service became memorable for all the wrong reasons. He could never get over the break in the familiar structure in his mind. In that flight cabin, the air hostess' response made him cry uncontrollably. A full-blown meltdown followed. Both Pia and I felt helpless. What an end to that holiday in Rome!

This was one of those moments of truth that unfailingly brought on feelings of guilt. I wish I had had the presence of mind to prepare him adequately before the flight. Upon arriving at Gatwick airport in London, Noel had recovered somewhat. As we settled into the cab, he looked at me with a puzzled expression and asked in broken sentences, 'Baba, how did the air hostess know I had eaten ten croissants for breakfast at Tirreno Hotel?' This insight into his innate, wonderful capability of trying to reconcile with an adverse situation through his own way of reasoning was very exciting. This could help build a fairly nuanced strategy that catalyses the process of reconciliation, thus coping with trauma and confusion. It charged me up, injecting fresh energy into my approach. I felt that there was a light that showed the way to induct him into a very simple 'solution-based structure'—that there were possibilties of introducing him to abstract notions of 'good luck' and 'bad luck', associations that he could comprehend, thus helping him cope with adverse outcomes and recognise wins as well.

When things work out the way you want them to, that is 'good luck' and 'bad luck' when things do not go as per expectation. I said, 'It had nothing to do with you, Noel. So don't be upset. Life is random, so what's important is how you respond.' This was the core teaching that I had to transfer to Noel to arm him with a tool that he could use.

Noel would get very agitated, disproportionately so, with disappointing situations. For example, one day, on our regular jaunt to the shawarma kebab shop in the PVR Saket area, we found that the shop had closed down for renovation. Noel's tension arose—endless crying and frustration that knew no bounds. It pushed me to work out a strategy to replace the disappointment with another lucid structure based on a linear thought, somewhat easy for him to understand, that could pacify him following the breaking of an existing structure. When disappointment made its appearance, I used the prompt, 'Noel, this is bad luck!' instead of a complex explanation of why something was not going to plan. First, I would give him a learnt label (bad luck) and allow a little time for everything to sink in. Then I would proceed with reasons for the situation such as, 'Noel, the kebab shop is closed because it is going through renovation.' Renovation was not a word he understood. It was a new concept for him, a new label. Then I would move to explain the word 'renovation' in simple words framed within one or two sentences that he could connect with.

As we faced each day fraught with uncertainties and broken structures, this became the strategy—replace a rupture with a lucid, logical and simple linear structure. When Noel turned twenty, his self-initiated structure was, 'There is always a next time,' which had become his new tool to cope with disappointments. It was a joy to see this metamorphose into a positive feature of Noel's personality.

It must be said that tackling disappointments is an important intervention in the early development of a child. The autistic mind cannot be left to cope with disappointments as if they were the usual run of life. A deliberate strategy must be shaped, be it for a small child or an adult. Embedded in an excellent strategy is also the proactive handling of distress and all kinds of behavioural issues associated with disappointments. In the following chapter, I will illustrate another kind of strategy—replacing a hardened structure with modes of distraction and eventually shaping the replacement into a new structure that becomes enjoyable for all involved while developing it into a learning technique as well.

––––––

Post 9/11, the security frisking at the airports, shopping mall entrances, events, shows and so on, had become a part and parcel of life. Noel had to be carefully coached to stand still with his arms raised and it was very difficult for him to understand the reasons for this mandatory act. But he went along with it and learnt to wait. Then came a time when, in dazzling self-assuredness and an unusually buoyant tone, he'd ask while being frisked, 'Guard ji, can you also scratch my back?'

––––––

In September 2014, while everybody else was pleased about New Delhi airport going silent, sadness had descended in Noel's world. Half the thrill of travel for him was the ceaseless announcements of arrivals and departures of various flights over the PA system in the airport. The notion of an unknown voice trying to get hold of your attention and telling you so loudly what you are supposed to do was exciting for him.

His favourite line was: kripiya dhyaan dijiye (kindly pay attention)! The announcement brought back memories of his teacher's courteous yet commanding tone. At the airport, it was not only him, but the entire population around him that was being addressed by that firm, no-nonsense tone, and everybody was expected to comply. This amused Noel to no end.

––––––

We all daydream. However, Noel's manner of doing so was quite different. He discussed them, oblivious of any social unease that this may cause to others around him. Once his mother and sister were getting ready to travel to Dubai on vacation, they were to stay at my younger sister Chaitali's place. Noel would not be going, but he kept daydreaming that he was part of the holiday crew.

'See, I have cut all my nails, the security check at Dubai airport will not stop me,' he'd tell others. He had never been to Dubai, but he had overheard us talking about the airport's strictness. He discussed endlessly how he would go around with Pishi (my sister) and Pesho (my brother-in-law) in their BMW, chat with his cousins, sing his favourite Beatles songs for them, play with Bossy (their small, beautiful, fluffy dog) and so on.

He also wondered, with much anxiousness, if Bossy would come to fetch him from the airport: 'Bossy amaye airport theke nitey ashbey, ami jani.'

Then came a new twist to his narrative. 'Baba, I will not come back to Delhi from Dubai. I will stay in Dubai forever,' he said.

'In Pishi's house?' I asked tentatively. 'What will you do there?'

Noel answered with an overdose of confidence, 'I will get a job at Pizza Hut in Dubai.'

Noel was then an intern at Pizza Hut in Delhi. Hence, that presumption was not entirely misplaced.

'Noel, you silly boy, you will miss mum and baba, how can you stay without us?'

'I will do Skype call, Baba, I will not miss you and mum at all,' he said. I can still recall how riled up I felt at this.

CHAPTER FOUR

I Am Speaking to a Stranger, See, See!

Noel (then twelve) and I were at the Kolkata airport. We were scheduled to catch a flight to London to join Pia and Ahvana for the summer holidays. While I was busy checking my documents before submission, Noel kept ambling into 'no-go zones' such as the immigration officer's cubicle, crossing the security check without the mandatory frisking or sauntering into a snack bar. So, it was a peculiar kind of anxiety that swirled in my head—keeping a close watch on Noel for the entire time at the airport required the focus of a batsman facing a fast bowler; a steadfast eye coupled with on-the-edge reflexes. However, it was difficult for me to sustain that focus for several hours till we got to our seats on the aeroplane.

As I dropped into my seat finally and shut my eyes, a deep sigh of relief escaped me. I was in the middle and Noel had the privilege of the window seat. He appeared to be fascinated by the safety instruction manual and was calm and quiet, absorbed by the illustrations and graphics.

So, things were peaceful after all the hustle-bustle until an English gentleman, with much contentment written on his face, slid into his window seat in the row ahead of ours. The peace was shattered when, within a few minutes, the man turned around angrily and shot at me, 'Tell him to stop that! Right now!' I looked down and noticed that Noel was kicking the front seat ahead of him with his foot. He was enjoying the rhythmic kicking that went 'thud! thud!' and simply refused to stop.

I tried the usual parental strategies of distracting him with things that he found more interesting, but nothing seemed to work. Then I bent over and held Noel's legs firmly to prevent him from kicking and for him to get the message that it was not acceptable. However, he just waited for me to give up and started again.

It was a five-and-a-half-hour flight to London. How would I handle this? I was gripped by the fear of social reprimand and insult. It had to be stopped. I hammered him with the ultimate verbal threat that harried parents often resort to: 'Noel, you will be de-boarded from the plane!' However, it did not work. That familiar twinge of pain inside me, one of humiliation and defeat, began to slowly erupt beneath my outwardly calm composure.

The other intense feeling was guilt because of the threats and warnings that I had spewed to control the innocent boy. I knew it was wrong and unfair of me to behave that way.

You cannot justify any threats issued to stop a kid from doing what is harmless. Noel's actions were undertaken with utmost innocence. He had no insight into our ever-so-complicated ways of behaviour in public spaces.

Basic social behaviour in public spaces that most people handle in a swift and natural way eluded him. One could say that Noel was deeply impaired in the subject of social skills. Or another way of seeing this is that Noel was a different kind of boy. He felt free and could not understand why, as long as he was not hurting anyone, people were so unaccepting of his fun and trivial actions; he could not fathom how his gentle kicking that produced a musical sound similar to a drum beat was unacceptable social behaviour. Why would this be such a grave situation? Why would this be the cause of so much annoyance to the grandfatherly gentleman?

Books by experts on autism describe this social dimension as the most complex area of impairment in most children on the spectrum. It interferes with their way of understanding the world or interpreting its conventions and raises steep barriers in functional, academic, social and skill learning.

What I would want to underline here is that the recalibration of expectations from the child in the social space by the parents also needs to be addressed. They must objectively re-evaluate their reactions. An inner strength to handle the outside world's gaze must be developed; the discriminatory remarks and rebukes that come along the way must be swallowed. It's important to realise early that these are everyday life occurrences and there is likely to be no escape. Parents have to start working on themselves to prevent an early burnout. Parents just cannot afford a burnout! It is not an option!

Another perspective is that while we say it is an impairment of the disabled child, let us also look at Noel's behaviour from a non-typical lens, excluding what we refer to as an impairment, and analyse. The nature of his unapologetic free-spiritedness, his pervasive sense of being naturally insulated from the fear of social reprimand, gave him a hidden strength. We had to recognise that nuance and leverage that as well when we trained him for the social space. Our 'different' kind of boy could swiftly break down stilted barriers effortlessly with ease and humour. Noel's heart swelled with warmth, empathy and openness with people. To value, respect and cherish such attributes in your child is also an important characteristic to nurture as parents.

One evening, after I got back from work, Noel, then sixteen, cajoled me for an ice cream treat for his good work at home. We drove to a market in Greater Kailash. I was harbouring the idea of motivating the boy to enter the ice cream shop alone, handle the exchange with the shopkeeper and make the purchase himself.

Throughout his adolescence, it was evident that he had come to realise the notion of a social framework and the constant expectations that hinged on it. By this stage, we had found that some things were intuitively acceptable to him and that some things were not. However, he was not always sure when it was a new situation and was sometimes prone to reluctance. This time, however, I encouraged him and watched him walk up to the ice cream shop. He stood at the shop, spoke a few words across the counter, then suddenly turned around and briskly headed back.

I had stopped the car in the exit lane of the market. The street lights were dim, so I could not see Noel's face. I just heard him say, 'Baba, I am not feeling confident.' I could see the silhouette of the boy leaning on the bonnet, looking quite composed. This act might seem ordinary when seen through the prism of the neurotypical world. However, for the father of a neurodivergent child, this was a thrilling moment filled with anticipation. Here was self-initiated 'social' communication that was conceptually apt and accompanied by meaningful labelling of how he felt (not confident). Aha, that was a win!

I parked the car and stepped out. I accompanied the boy this time to the ice cream stall to assist him in the purchase. Noel felt reassured and confident with me around. He went through the steps and completed the task as I had taught him: thanking the stall sales attendant, collecting the balance and the bill from the shopkeeper and reflexively handing them to me.

Seeing him quite satisfied with this partially independent act, I suggested that he enjoy his treat while we walk across to the open air gym for some exercise. Noel did not like the idea. He never liked the idea of eating anything while walking. His argument was that since eating was such an enjoyable thing to do, then why must one reduce the pleasure by engaging in another activity such as walking or, for that matter, chatting? I fathomed as much without him articulating it.

He wanted to go inside any cafe, any restaurant and sit more comfortably in a proper chair to eat the ice cream that he had just bought. Tersely, I said that it was not possible to do so. Noel, in an agitated manner, persisted with his demand. He had sighted, through the transparent fascia of the restaurant nearby, many tables and chairs that lay unoccupied. Why couldn't he just go in, sit and eat his ice cream when so many seats were empty inside the restaurant? I explained the social rule of how one cannot eat something in a restaurant when one had purchased food from outside.

Noel appeared to think that I was making this up just because I was in no mood to give my approval to his plan. He was visibly upset. A full-blown tantrum erupted in the market. The thrill of the win just minutes before quickly evaporated, to be replaced by dismay. He continued to say the same thing, oscillating between an aggressive tone and a weepy one infused with self-pity, insisting the reason I'd offered was nonsensical.

Then, as we walked down the pavement in an agitated state, he spotted a door of a private house ajar. Noel quickly entered the house and seated himself on the staircase in the entranceway. With single-minded focus, he started licking his ice cream. After giving him a few minutes to savour it, I resumed my explanation that he could not possibly sit on some unknown person's staircase. 'It is simply not done!' I exclaimed in a fairly irritated tone, as I was running out of patience.

He then said in a flat tone (what he had heard a hundred times from me), 'Not socially acceptable?' And then kept parroting my constant objection, 'Not socially acceptable! Not socially acceptable!' He found my explanations bizarre. Why could he not rest on an empty staircase? What kind of rules were these?

How does it matter if we did not know the occupants of the house? What about the salon on the opposite side—it had very comfortable seats that were empty. He could see that through the big glass window. He wanted to go there now. Why couldn't he? The free-spirited boy found these social rules illogical and irksome. He had a sense of self that would not bend easily to another's command because he genuinely did not see the answer to the question, 'Why should I do this or not do that?' He had his own configuration of what should be important. It dawned upon me that fighting this configuration was futile. It also opened my eyes to respecting him more, giving him the space to undo my objections and for me to deliberately tone them down.

There were disruptive episodes through his teens when Noel would scream his head off in shops as if the world was going to collapse. I always ended up mumbling some explanation to the staff to get out of such situations. Sometimes, the people around were considerate and sporting, but many a time, they were rude and glared endlessly, almost as if to say, 'Your son is extremely spoilt! A hopeless case!'

This kind of unpredictable, unruly behaviour can be psychologically draining for parents and caregivers. One has to be conscious of not reflexively succumbing to the use of corporal punishment, intimidation, threats and humiliation. These were options that were standard operating procedures for earlier generations, but are not widely acceptable today, having been replaced by self-disciplining and mindfulness on the part of parents.

There are also people who would, without knowing much about autism, say: 'Don't worry, sir, *kuch nahi hoga*, just let him be.' This would assuage and win our hearts over with incredible ease.

At the sports club, occasionally, Noel would want to strike up a conversation with complete strangers. 'Hello! How are you?' This was his loud, warm, shout-out to fellow walkers on the track or to the other learners on the tennis court or at shopping malls.

The instant reaction from his mother or me would be, 'Noel, you are not allowed to talk to strangers. They will get irritated,' or 'We don't say hello to strangers, got it?' Noel used to reply with an affirmative, 'Got it!' though he found it funny. 'Why irritated when they are greeted?' he would ask in his broken, expressive speech. It also became a trick to tease us at will. If we ignored the shout-out to strangers and did not say anything to stop him, he would prompt us mockingly. 'Baba, I am speaking to a stranger, see, see!' he would say, with amusement and a knowing glitter in his eyes. Social niceties were put on the dock and laughed at.

Our strategy changed as he crossed twenty—we let him talk to strangers and also forced ourselves to join him in brief exchanges of social pleasantries with such people. But then came another stumbling block. Noel would walk away abruptly, as he could never hold a conversation. He had adequate verbal abilities to express himself to a considerable extent but lacked the capability to have a two-way conversation that neurotypical folks so intuitively engage in. Otherwise, daily social interactions vis-à-vis autism are indeed a minefield and a person unaware of the aspects of the condition would infer that Noel was very rude and surely raised badly. One just hoped that the other person in the conversation was blessed with a good sense of humour.

In another situation, while boarding a flight at the Delhi airport, Noel's response to the air hostess' customary, 'Welcome on board, sir' was an equally cordial, 'How are you, air hostess? How is your stomach? My stomach is not good today.' I quickly nudged him forward to cut short the embarrassment and diverted him by asking him to look for his seat number.

In the middle of any sophisticated social gathering, Noel's valiant attempts to mingle meant the deployment of his automated set of questions: 'What is your name? Where do you stay? Do you have any songs on your mobile?' After which, it was quite possible for him to break into a full-fledged monologue about the toilet.

Even though Noel was toilet-trained (after considerable hardship in those initial years), he knew it was a weapon to generate attention and the hoopla around it assured him some entertainment. He did not grasp the aspect of it being age-appropriate or not. What happened when he had a bathroom-related accident? Where did it happen the last time? I would be close to collapsing with embarrassment. The entire business of visiting a washroom and its myriad themes is so fascinating if you care to see them through his lens. Intertwined with other physiological, emotional and sensory experiences inevitably made it a monstrous, multi-dimensional subject. For example, the discomfort in the stomach with a meal gone wrong could bring on a host of self-directed concerns, insecurities, fears, guilt and confusion. For someone who cannot analyse that and communicate it to another person coherently, it could play havoc on the mind and possibly manifest in expressions and mood swings that would be interpreted as 'odd behaviour' in ordinary parlance.

Stomach problems affect each one of us and somewhere there is always a side-effect on our mood. We know how to deal with that in a social context. How much to talk about a digestion problem and whom to talk about it with; what quick therapies or remedies can be taken and so on. We learn this naturally as we grow older.

What did help was to encourage Noel to speak freely, at least, to one or two close, everyday companions or caregivers. To coach him with gentle 'How you are feeling?' questions or easy language labels that described various states of discomfort, i.e., 'I am feeling uneasy in my stomach', 'I have overeaten so I am feeling uncomfortable', 'I feel like going to the loo often', 'Stomach issues happen to everybody, not just Noel' and so forth, are examples of some of the expressions that were inserted in his verbal inventory. Pretty much like chatbot-automated responses, which are pre-planned for likely questions in today's digital interfaces!

Waiting for his order to be served in a restaurant, Noel tended to get impatient. When he would notice the waiter who'd taken our order hustling past our table with another table's food, he would invariably call out to them, 'Here, here, serve it here!' causing discomfort all around, while Noel remained pleasantly unaware of the social unease he'd caused.

We had to rewind and course correct ever so often in the area of social teaching. Something comes up all of a sudden and then you realise the gaps that exist even within a good social teaching initiative. Here is one observation that bolsters my point. It was dark when we were walking out of the overcrowded market of Alakananda in South Delhi. A stray cow was standing in the parking lot with no intention of moving, blocking the way. As I managed to wriggle my way through, I turned back and saw a twenty-year-old Noel pleading with the cow like a true gentleman, politely and patiently, 'Cow, hello cow! Please excuse me, I have to get to my car.'

Instead of navigating his way intuitively, he started having an earnest conversation as he had been taught to with people around. It was rote learning in a generalised way.

Social dimensions encompass the understanding and handling of the self when faced with common emotional urges laced with physical wants, such as temptations. We all learn very early in life how to curb our temptations. Self-restraint does not come easily to most, so, as one would expect, it was quite difficult for Noel. This is possibly true for many in the neurodivergent community.

The temptation of exciting and tasty food, for instance. I noticed that it was not just the taste of food or simply the whetting of appetite that excited Noel. It was also the feel of his mouth being overfilled. The ladoo, the rassogolla, a bun, or a lemon tart were not to be bitten into but placed into his mouth in one go. The sensation of a full mouth appeared to be a stimulation that he enjoyed, a sort of sensorial high.

On my regular business trips to Amritsar, when Noel was in his late teens, I loved bringing boondi ladoos from Bansal's, a famous sweet shop. It was such a joy to watch Noel pick up a big boondi ladoo and put it in his mouth and then chew on it like a camel with utmost concentration. The challenge was to get him to stop eating after one or two pieces!

When a casserole of exciting food such as a pizza or a cake or an assortment of kebabs was placed on the dining table in a restaurant or at home, Noel had a tendency to pick up an extra helping from the casserole after everyone had been served. But then there was an interesting breakthrough one day when he surprised us all by developing his own strategy for dealing with familiar temptations. He simply picked up the casserole with the remaining pieces, walked straight to the kitchen and left it there. Noel's interesting solution was to remove it from his line of sight entirely. It was a prudent way of dealing with the temptation of food. Wise people often say it is better to avoid temptations in the first place than to struggle to resist them, but for an autistic person to frame this abstract thought in his mind, by way of pro-action, would qualify as a breakthrough!

The Maxim bakery outlet in Kailash Colony market in the neighbourhood was a place where Noel was always warmly greeted by smiling faces. Noel would always look with wide eyes at the mouth-watering merchandise on display behind the brightly lit glass and then would ask his sister if he could get one of the cakes. She would have already bought cookies for him, so she would refuse. Noel would move closer to the glass, lean forward, look wistfully at the fancy cakes and then suddenly shut his eyes tightly. Taut lines would form on his face; you could see that he was making a great effort to conquer his temptation!

Often, Noel would conclude that expressions of frustration in real-life situations, by TV news anchors or a politician making a theatrical speech should be labelled 'sad'. Unable to comprehend the exact feeling based on facial expressions, 'sad' was the default label that he resorted to. If I were to transliterate his intent, it would imply that the 'person is troubled'. Any kind of facial manifestation of being troubled was 'feeling sad' and Noel's reaction would be, 'Baba, let's help them!' The expressive language labelling limitations were evident, but his empathy levels were high, without a doubt.

Further, various non-verbal gestures and social signals—holding hands, arms around the shoulder, a hug, pat on the back were, by and large, missing from his socially limited repertoire. But through continuous reinforcement, they started appearing in Noel little by little.

One evening, as I watched a BBC documentary about Margot Wallstrom, my son hovered around me, seeking my attention. In a friendly tone, I directed him to watch the film with me and to generate interest, I started providing a bit of commentary in my specially-styled-for-Noel way. This meant I regulated my voice, articulated things slowly and chose simple, commonly used words in English or Bengali.

'Noel, see, this is the Foreign Minister ... of a country named Sweden ... she is brave and confident (Noel's top-of-the-mind words) ... her office is in the capital city, Stockholm, like Delhi is the capital city of ...? Yes, India!'

The documentary had prolonged sequences of Wallstrom at various conferences at international locations, receiving heaps of large flower bouquets. Noel watched intently and then asked in earnest, 'Do they have no flowers in Stockholm?' It bowled me over! Such social gestures mystified Noel and were wasted on him.

Another instance to recount was when he was promised by my brother-in-law, Noel's Ranjit da and my elder sister, Mitali (Noel's Boro pishi) that they would accompany him to the Volkswagen showroom. As Noel quietly waited in the corner seat, there were a lot of animated conversations in the living room. The tea was being drunk at a languid pace. Noel was growing impatient. He asked once again, 'When are we going to the Volkswagen showroom?' He got the same reply from Ranjit da, 'We will leave after we all finish drinking tea.' Peeved, Noel rose swiftly and drank up the remaining tea in each of the cups, first from his Boro pishi's teacup, then one after the other—there were about seven of us—so he finished seven cups pronto! Once he'd finished, he announced loudly, 'All the tea is finished! Now we can go!' This left all of us flabbergasted. After a momentary shock, loud laughter followed.

As we've seen, in Noel's case, learning social cues through intuition was not a possible pathway. In his teens and early twenties, Noel's inventory of structures drawn from actual experiences appeared to have been cast. If there was a sudden or unannounced change in the situational context that would require subtle navigation, Noel would be immobilised. The hiatus in social-related comprehension was always there. He registered something so directly, innocently and linearly that his responses always aroused curiosity and brought on a chuckle along with an unfailingly warm appreciation of his endearingly different mind.

––––––––

Noel, at nineteen, had learnt to cut his nails all by himself. It was indeed a bolt from the blue that morning! We had all given up on this long ago and had stopped bothering him because we knew he was unable to manage the clippers due to his fine motor coordination challenge.

The compelling force that got him completely focused turned out to be his new presumption that the security guards who run such a thorough check at the airports may stop him and that any travel plans to Kolkata may get jeopardised unless his fingernails were cut.

His fine motor coordination challenge was surmounted in one big sweep. It was entirely attributable to his self-reasoning and self-motivation. Another breakthrough came up rather soon; his ability to shave with an electric shaver immaculately. Slender rewards such as these are enough to prompt a celebration on Planet Autism.

––––––––

'Well, Noel, you've not been a gentleman this week at all,' I said rather crossly once. 'You've been speaking far too loudly, your writing was not up to the usual mark and your hands have been positively dirty even after you washed them. What do you have to say?'

Noel was quiet. Then, in a matter-of-fact tone, he piped up, 'OLX pe bech de (Sell me on OLX).' OLX is a widely-known second-hand goods e-platform.

I tried to keep a straight face but it was not possible. I threw my head back and laughed.

CHAPTER FIVE

Let's Just Chat

Noel had turned nineteen but he was still not capable of figuring out the goings-on in any team game; things such as the rules, the appreciation of tactics and teamwork were a mystery to him. He was not sure why winning was so much better than losing! Why was there such a brouhaha about leading with a certain number of goals scored or why was winning a match such a spectacular deal? This was perceptible from his attitude when he took part in competitive swimming or racing events himself. After much lucid explanation of what winning means (essentially, getting ahead of others) I would often say tersely, 'Noel, please go out and win the race.' It was my habitual clarion call, but it was abstract mumbo jumbo for him.

I just wanted to fill his life with a multiplicity of outdoor sporty experiences, just as I had in my years growing up. My whole mission was to put him in the midst of new experiences, so that he could learn and enjoy a wide variety of things, just like any other boy his age. It was a joy to see how Noel interpreted and reacted in every such situation that I drew him into. His way of seeing our world was just so different, thought-provoking and amusing that it often gave us fresh new perspectives about the ordinary things around us that would have never crossed my head.

I started to take him to watch big matches. On one occasion, it was the Hockey Men's Final (Olympics 2012 Qualifier) at the Dhyan Chand National Hockey Stadium in Delhi. It was going to be a night match under the floodlights. Being inside a stadium was sheer joy for Noel and he wore a big smile right through the day, filled with anticipation and excitement. Holding Noel's hand, I walked through the crowds towards the gallery seats in the stadium. The hype prior to the game, the giant digital scoreboard with all its psychedelic gimmicks, loud music, countdowns, wild cheering and so forth contributed to a festive mood that he enjoyed. I was initially concerned about his reaction to the noise since he had the characteristic autistic sensory overload issue and had been uncomfortable with loud sounds since his childhood. He was often distressed in public places because of loud sounds until he crossed his late teens. However, lately, he appeared to have adjusted himself to high-decibel sounds around him as he never complained or showed any signs of discomfort. Pia and I concluded that his coping abilities had improved in this area.

That was an immensely positive step.

At half-time, Noel pleaded for a bottle of Cola. This was an indulgence that he was rarely allowed owing to the high sugar content, even though he argued that Cola was like juice and therefore, not off limits for him. His logic was that if Cola was 'not okay', why were juices displayed in visually similar bottles and in the same shops? It must mean Cola is a juice and thus, healthy. He harboured a strong feeling that we actually did not have a good enough reason for restraining him from the fun of having Cola and was always resentful about this.

In order to give him a tangible reason to hold on to, I taught him about the notion of hyperactivity. 'Cola is to be avoided because it produces hyperactivity, Noel,' I had told him. He had caught onto the significance of the phrase after I had acted out hyperactivity for him.

This led to a heartwarming and delightful moment at Ahvana's eighteenth birthday party, where she and her friends, around fifteen of them, were chattering away in the living room with loud music playing. Noel was being put through the social drill of asking guests what drinks they would like, followed by serving them individually using a tray. He was going around asking everyone in his characteristically earnest tone, 'What drink would you like to have?' He finished the round and was striding out of the room when suddenly, he halted in his tracks, turned the volume of the music system down and stood at the door so that everyone could hear him loud and clear. 'All of you want Cola, all will get hyperactivity!' he declared. The chatter came to an abrupt halt and then everyone erupted into laughter. Social grace was shattered, but it made for a gawkily cheerful moment!

To come back to the hockey match, India was leading with

a score of 6 - 1 and I was, like every other spectator, thrilled to bits. I conceded to the demand for a Cola at break time. We trudged along, looking for a stall inside the stadium, but there wasn't one. He was immensely disappointed, but I reassured and promised him that I would get him the drink after the game. That did not seem to pacify him and he remained unsettled, repeating every few minutes, 'Please, please give me a Cola.'

However, I took my mind off it and refused to be distracted from the game. After the match, as we were trooping out of the stadium, I bought him the promised drink at a paanwaala's shop outside the stadium and we got into the car to get home. He did not look pleased. Instead, he kept sipping the soda but also continued whining, 'Please give me a Cola, Baba.'

I had delivered on my promise, so what was the problem? I was close to giving him a scolding. How could the fellow sipping a Cola keep asking me for one at the same time? I tried to reason with him, but nothing helped. He started to sob. I sensed an impending meltdown.

After a few quiet moments, realisation struck me. Around two years ago, Noel and I had come to see a hockey match at the same stadium and I had bought him a Cola *inside* the stadium premises and he had consumed the drink *inside* the stadium. But I had not done so this time and that was the source of his distress. No autism book could have taught me the hold of structure in situations like this.

Whatever had happened last in that situational context had become the rigidly preset structure, even if it had been two years since. So, the fun of having a Cola was gone when bought from outside the stadium. Instead, his frustration and tantrums had set in with the mighty force of a twister. Although Noel was verbal, he could not articulate the cause of his distress. My take was that a fixed recurring event kept his mind focused and stable, giving him a sense of control and calm. Any change would induce a feeling of helplessness and extreme unease, working him up to an outburst.

The additional challenge was that he could not express his feelings in words, not even in a general way. This was very surprising because, given his verbal abilities, this seemed a reasonable expectation.

Such was the puzzling nature of his condition that the joining of the dots was a form of mental gymnastics that I would intuitively slip into. The myriad manifestations of this bewildering appetite for structure and its perennial pervasiveness in the lives of individuals with autism are both a challenge and also a way to open up opportunities for learning in inventive ways. Needless to add, the learning is never over. So, the conventional yardstick of age becomes irrelevant. The point then is that parents or caregivers have to step out of the familiar shell of cause-effect rational thinking into a new non-logical space to be able to shape learning and social behaviour strategies that benefit the child in the long term. This is a continuous process. And certainly not an easy one!

Examining closely the all-encompassing phenomenon of structure opens the floodgates to big ideas. But this entails considerable patience and imagination to convert them into solid foundational teaching strategies.

I have described one kind of strategy for the replacement of a hardened structure in the previous chapter. I will now describe another replacement strategy via positive distraction (that does not involve an object inducement).

Noel had a busy schedule through the weekdays. Even after school hours, there was a regular line-up of activities for him—tennis, swimming, occupational therapy sessions at an OT clinic and vocal music lessons. The downside was that he never enjoyed his Sundays and the stipulated holidays because the departure from his weekday schedule made him very unsettled, unhappy and restless. So unusual! Sundays for him were days of tension rather than of rest, relaxation and enjoyment. As the years rolled by through his teens and early twenties, this changed in a positive way. He started looking forward to Sundays as a break from his routine; an important milestone was accomplished! But how?

The positive turnabout was made possible because Pia and Ahvana had devised a method to ease him into Sundays and other holidays, which was sparked by saying, 'Let's chat about Kolkata.' It was an activity he'd begun to enjoy; one that was fixed at a certain time and place.

He would be taken to the walking track in the sports complex. As soon as he would step onto it, he would start as if an automated switch had come on and always began by announcing, 'We will chat about Kolkata now!' Ahvana would then ask him, 'Noel, what are your plans for Kolkata?' and he would respond with details about the places he would want to eat at, which of his favourite Bengali sweet shops he'd visit, plans for golf practice at Tolly Club, which exciting treats his grandparents would lay out for him, what movie he was planning to watch at the nearby hall and so on. Interestingly, as soon as he reached the end of his walk on the track, he would stop talking about Kolkata. The switch had to go off instantly. An unusual twist, yes. You could not resume the conversation in the car once he'd left the walking track or after everyone got home. Noel would not participate. He would be wordless—absolutely quiet. Talking about Kolkata outside of that walking track would mean going beyond the confines of the newly defined structure!

Whenever a visit to Kolkata was being planned, Noel would request a toy car and bridge. That had been a set pattern since he was eight. Every time, at the start of each journey, it had to be a new bridge set! We were only too happy to make that purchase since it allowed Noel to remain calm and emotionally secure on the train and cut down on his stims of loud self-talk or hard claps.

When he grew older, I grew a little worried about his request for toy cars and would respond with, 'Noel, you are eighteen now, a grown man. You cannot ask for a toy bridge! It was okay when you were a small boy.' I even tried to steer him towards something that seemed more age-appropriate, that would gradually ease off the early childhood obsessions and replace them. Then I realised that his request emanated from a need to cling to familiar objects to deal with the associated anxiety of train travel; a self-soothing remedy.

I began to question our way of thinking, which was so clearly based on a rational thought process conditioned by the way we expected things to happen, applicable to conventions or norms—we refused to see any other way of relating to the fixations that were survival necessities for Noel. It was actually our perceptual block and this was the part where we had to work on ourselves.

We had to step out of that straitjacketed thinking of 'age appropriateness'. Pia, Ahvana and I had to free ourselves from this boxed-in state of mind. We had to re-condition ourselves and feel perfectly okay about our lanky eighteen-year-old boy looking at a toy car and a toy bridge, fixated for hours, studying the details minutely, sitting quietly on his window seat in the speeding train.

Noel's repertoire of rigid interests had expanded over time to include watching YouTube, spending time on the iPad, going through old family photo albums and glossy magazines and listening to music. However, these could not displace his obsessive attachment to the toy car and bridge set of his younger days when it came to a train journey.

That the toy car and bridge set fixation belonged to a certain stage of his childhood was a concept that was hard for him to comprehend. In that sense, some patterns, rigid structures, were life-stage agnostic. It was up to us to accept them with dignity. What should be accepted as life-stage agnostic or what should be replaced with a new structure or when to loosen up an existing structure is a call that parents have to make.

For instance, the discomfort and frustration that Noel felt on my coming home earlier than the normal time (mentioned in a previous chapter) was something I wanted to change. I decided to figure out ways of offsetting that rigidness of structure. I began to force myself to come out of the end-of-day tiredness, switch on a button and turbocharge myself into becoming all boisterous, to the point of dazzling my son. As I came through the door, I would do silly acts to catch him by surprise and distract him from his anguish. I would jump up and down, do cartwheels, break into dance steps, sing out loud and gingerly arm-wrestle with him, accompanied by loud cheering so that he was overwhelmed.

Eventually, my untimely arrival from the office was greeted by a tall, handsome, twenty-five-year-old Noel, standing at the door, full of extraordinary warmth and his signature ear-to-ear grin: 'Hiya dad! You are back!' He had overcome the stumble of transition to my sudden appearance. It may be hard to believe but it had taken years to bring about this change.

———

Ahvana was arriving post-midnight at Delhi International Airport Terminal 3. I passed on this message early in the evening to the hyper and anxious brother who was keen to receive her. I also added that I would wake him up so he could accompany me to the airport, even if it was going to be at an unearthly hour.

'So please chill and go to sleep, Noel,' I told him. He'd already asked me over a hundred times in the past two days if he could receive her at the airport. He had evidently missed her a lot for that one week that she had been away, holidaying in Dubai.

As I woke to the alarm and swiftly got ready, I came across an unusual sight once I switched on the entrance area light. Noel had chosen to sleep by the side of the main door on the floor, making sure I could not reach the main door without crossing over him, lest I forget to call him or perhaps even deliberately 'forget' and make up an excuse later. The brother-sister bond had remained strong over the years after all.

CHAPTER SIX

Swim and Sing

'Noel cannot learn swimming. I have tried many techniques with him but he is making no progress,' said the top-notch swimming coach at a posh club in Kolkata in a defeated tone. I looked away, disappointed and sipped my lime soda. On the outside, I attempted to look calm and cool but within, I was being crushed by an all-too-familiar downward spiral of quiet surrender.

That agonising surrender filled up every bit of breathing tissue inside me and I could barely talk about it to even my closest friend. I still had to show that I was tough and could take it all in my stride. Conventional wisdom dictates that you show acceptance and counsels you to appear nonchalant when there is no progress even after intently pursuing a specific goal for years with your child. You have to appear blasé to the external world. Every child is different, after all. To arm oneself with such an attitude is ideal. The arguments are rational and constructive, experts would say. But my question deep-down has always been: What about the turbulence inside? What about the dagger that continues to twist inside you? No blood, no visible gashes, simply unbearable pain.

At that stage of fatherhood, this is the darkness which was the hardest to bear.

My gaze went towards a six-year-old Noel, splashing gleefully and chuckling away in the shallow side of the pool. It was a picture of unbridled happiness. Juxtapose this image with the familiar gloomy narrative from so many who had attempted teaching Noel: 'Noel cannot learn this' or 'Noel cannot make it' or 'Please understand, he is not normal!' and so forth. Such lines unfailingly pierced the heart, bringing upon a sense of helplessness.

My wife, Pia, an excellent swimmer, had brought him along to the pool with her since he was three. Initially, it was a joy watching him play in the pool in the safety of the shallow side, splashing water with his hands rapidly. He loved doing so and remained oblivious to the irritation that he caused others, which were more often than not grumpy adults and not the small children taking swimming lessons. Because of this, we got embarrassed every time we went, but nothing we said to Noel would stop him from splashing water for the entire forty-five minutes that we were in the swimming pool.

The years rolled by. Noel turned ten and nothing changed. Those unstoppable antics in the pool remained. The glares, rebukes and awkward stares did not discourage him. However, we never stopped taking him to the pool and appointed several coaches to teach Noel, but one by one, they gave up. Each attempt lasted for two or three weeks. Then came along a friend, Subrata, who took up the daunting task.

Subrata possessed the most important attribute—tons of patience. Noel's steadfast non-compliance made no visible difference to him. He remained calm and collected. But Noel did not make any significant progress.

Pia, my wife, would try very hard to get him to fully stretch in the water. Then we would try together to move his arms and legs in a coordinated fashion, but to no avail. Noel would comply, but only for ten minutes and then the boy would insist on being left alone. He would return to his repetitious splashing, punctuated by his chuckles.

In the year 1998, we moved to Delhi. This meant a complete reorganisation and adaptation to a new city and a new home. In spite of all the explanations that were given to Noel about the change of city, in line with the advice mentioned in the parenting handbooks that I'd read, Noel appeared to be unsure. He felt this move was temporary. Almost every day, he woke up and asked about when we would return to Kolkata. He was unsure, but not distressed. He was accepting the changes around him rather well, including the switch from Bengali to Hindi as the predominantly spoken language.

It is perhaps a stroke of luck that we managed to procure what was going to be an important advantage for Noel: a permanent membership in the DDA (Delhi Development Authority) Siri Fort Sports Complex, an excellent sporting facility with a cricket field, encircled by a walking and jogging track, a golf driving range, a mini golf course, tennis courts, squash courts, a roller-skating rink, indoor and outdoor badminton and a splendid Olympic-sized swimming pool. I saw in all this an area of escape for Noel from the anxiety levels of everyday life, as well as an opportunity zone where he could commit to learning the sports of his choice.

Pia persisted with the swimming initiative with Noel in the Siri Fort pool. The ceaseless splashing continued at the pool for a long time, probably a year. Our resolve to take him to the pool, however, remained rock-solid.

Then one glorious day, as I entered the pool from the changing room, Pia pointed at him excitedly.

'Look at our boy!'

I spotted Noel in the deep end of the pool, floating with his head fully above the water, legs outstretched, his arms sliding backwards. There was also a lifeguard on duty, keeping a close watch on him. My instant reaction of fear subsided as I watched Noel from a distance. Jubilation soon took over. We had successfully climbed a steep mountain and just touched the peak.

A silver lining for all parents and caregivers of neurodivergent children is the fact that miracles do happen. Yes, they are few and far between, but they happen. That moment of elation is indescribable and remains embedded. When one of those miracles happens, the emotional high can eclipse all the personal triumphs that you may have experienced in your academic life or in your professional career. Noel had made it! He could swim independently. He had broken through the chains of sensorial overload and motor coordination that were integral to his condition. Instead of succumbing to social pressure, our resolve had paid off. Pia's drive and patience, along with her attitude of not allowing societal unease to ever come in the way, had created a space where we could try new things with Noel. He was now fully independent in the swimming pool. However, Noel showed no excitement at all—any other child would have been jubilant in that moment of success. To him, it all seemed business as usual.

My belief was that it would lead to an all-encompassing positive effect on Noel, physically and mentally, while furthering his desire for expressive communication. He was easy-going in his swimming style, had slow movements and a gentle forward action, always with a song on his lips. His all-time favourite was Celine Dion's *I Am Alive*. His take was that all the joy of swimming lay in doing so at a leisurely pace. The song, always sung aloud with gusto, added to that enjoyment. However, in the next three years, Noel learnt how to improve his speed and direction so that he could take part in the prestigious national competition: the Indian chapter of the Special Olympics.

We met Santosh, a soft-spoken yet enthusiastic professional swimming coach who worked with neurodiverse children and adults. He started coaching Noel in the swimming pool about thrice a week. Noel took a liking to Santosh—the bond was going to be important—so that was one big step forward. Santosh was sincere, protective and affectionate towards Noel.

Plenty of hard work and regularity yielded results and at sixteen, Noel was selected as part of a team that would represent

Delhi in a National Aquatics Meet under the aegis of Indian Special Olympics, hosted in Mumbai in 2009.

There was a meeting prior to the event in Delhi for all the parents, interested family members and caregivers concerning the necessary instructions for travel, lodging and other arrangements.

The participants would undertake an overnight train journey with some degree of supervision from the coaches and other administrators travelling to the event. My heart sank when I learnt of this. Noel would not be able to travel with the group. His impairments would not permit group travel.

The manager of the Delhi team, a senior swimming coach and a very pleasant man, took me aside and told me that it would be good as an overall team-building exercise for Noel to travel with them. His perspective came from dealing with neurodivergent and disabled children who did not have acute social anxieties and erratic moods. I remained hesitant. The complex array of challenges that I was taking into account belonged to a whole other level of difficulty—something that even people who are somewhat aware of the subject of autism would not comprehend.

Noel's need for structure, his frequent anxiety rushes and stim behaviours were nearly impossible to comprehend for others and his constant need to be calmed, especially at times of distress for no apparent reason, drove me to think of an alternative. I requested the team manager to exempt him from group travel and the planned stay in a college hostel in Mumbai. So, out of the entire team of fifteen from Delhi, Noel would be the only one who would travel and stay separately.

Staying at a hotel or a friend's place was ruled out. It would not be practical and Noel would have great difficulties adjusting. With a stroke of good fortune, as soon as I requested my new acquaintance, Mr Naga, who was an HR expert in the corporate world and lived in Los Angeles, to allow us to use his flat in the Malabar Hill area, I got an instant, 'Yes, of course, I will do anything for Noel.'

For me, this was a godsend! I had no words to describe my gratitude towards Mr Naga, whom I had befriended only a month ago.

We arrived at the Khar Gymkhana swimming pool, the venue for the elimination rounds. I was totally taken aback by the sheer size of the crowd. There were about three hundred people around and general pandemonium near the pool's seating area. There was a certain busyness all about that made Noel visibly nervous. While I attempted to soothe him, he spotted a snack counter on the poolside. Immediately, he began shoving aside people on his way to the stall, perhaps as an act of escape or a way to express his stress in this unfamiliar situation and, all of a sudden, he was trying to grab the sandwiches and pastries laid out on the kiosk's counter. With all my strength, I tried to hold him back, but to no avail. That is how the day started.

Noel then had to wait for hours in the waiting area next to the poolside before his ability and age grouping was announced. There was no other place that I could take Noel to that would be quiet enough for him to engage in some other activity by way of distraction. We continued to sit in the waiting section, anxious and discomfited, Noel tugging at the sleeve of his blue Delhi team jersey while I fumed silently.

After brooding for a while, my attention turned to the various participants of different age groups from various state teams—West Bengal, Karnataka, Tamil Nadu, Odisha and so on. There must have been only a handful of ASD children who had severe impairments in terms of communication and social behaviour and would probably be in the same zone as Noel in terms of general ability and communication levels. However, the remaining participants, around 150 of them, appeared to be high functioning with somewhat close to age-appropriate social communication skills. Many of them were busy speaking on their phones and chatting with accompanying teachers, coaches or other team members. In my mind, overfilled with autism issues, this ability appeared to be light years ahead of the communication capabilities Noel or the few other participants on the autism spectrum possessed.

It was such an unequal situation because competitiveness depends not just on the sporting skill in question but the general handling of the environment, the uncertainties, the social navigation, all the cognitive skills needed to comprehend what is going on and what is required of the competitor. This was a new area of learning for me. I would never have had this invisible curtain raised without becoming an autism dad. There were just a few outstation parents; most of the parents who turned up were from Mumbai. However, there were coaches, assistant coaches and coordinators from each state team. I plunged into a tornado of negative thoughts. I began wondering whether coming all the way and putting Noel through this hardship was of any real worth, given the unequal competitive scenario. Would Noel be able to focus amid the high noise levels? Would he comply at all?

My gloomy thoughts were suddenly broken by a shrill announcement on the PA system. The time had come after nearly a four-hour wait. Noel was chattering to himself; a fixed phrase came into his speech suddenly and it became a steady refrain. It was an echolalic speech tag. On a visit to England some years ago, he was fixated on a phrase, 'Space ... space!' He used to repeat it a thousand times, although it had no apparent meaning, when he felt things were confusing or he was not sure what would happen next. It was odd but a definitive expression of helplessness and acute anxiety. No, it did not mean the literal sense of wanting space. This repetitious verbalised expression could be classified as a coping mechanism. And at that moment, it had returned and erupted with intensity.

It then struck me that the boy did not fully comprehend the signal to begin: the whistle and the implication of the red flag being waved. To me, it was a bolt from the blue as I suddenly realised that we had missed teaching him about the 'start' signal. Noel appeared to be in a daze. There were five others in different lanes. They had all taken their positions. Each one's timings would be recorded and a shortlist would be made for the next elimination round the following day. After the elimination round, the final race would take place for various groups. I spoke animatedly to Noel, encouraging him to focus on the immediate fifty metres that he had to swim for the time-recorder. He seemed so distracted, a far more disadvantaged participant than the others. Seeing him so lost, the officials around clearly felt sorry for him and were probably certain that he would not go any further in the competition. I walked across to the organisers a minute before they were to begin the elimination race and pointed out that it would be fair to give the participants a rehearsal of the start signal. To expect all of them to be familiar with it and comply was unfair. They agreed. However, in reality, it was Noel and another participant who needed it the most amongst the eight participants. Others were much better clued in on the start signal, which was evident in the mock starts.

Even a little rehearsal works exceedingly well in a new setting. Noel responded to the start signal, though not instantaneously, and quickly gathered speed as he swam in his lane and finished with a time that qualified him for the next round. As we were leaving, there was an announcement that the venue for the next day would be on the Marina beach at the Mahindra corporate group's swimming club.

For me, the small relief and joy of Noel's moving into the second round was instantly washed away by this new development. I could not smile any more. Yet again, a new situation and a new set of variables would be thrust upon the poorly adjusted participants like Noel. However, this is how most sporting events and activities for disabled and neurodivergent individuals take place. Not that the organisers can be blamed; the awareness of this disability and the related issues is usually so low across the board.

The next day, we arrived at the new venue on Marina beach. It was a bright sunny day with a steady wind blowing across the sea. The swimming pool was much larger than the other venue, so it did not seem as crowded. There was plenty of place to sit along the sides of the pool. However, the open spaces in and around the pool did not help Noel at all, quite the opposite of my expectations. He appeared to have a breakdown and refused to participate in the second round. All the parents, coaches, participants and their siblings watched Noel in this state of despair, screaming endlessly, crying out, 'Space ... space!' I could see the pity in their eyes for the boy and his frazzled father. His refrain had clearly been triggered by the new venue. Such distress in the autistic mind is a huge puzzle. It's very difficult to reason and the despair can rise into a full-fledged meltdown.

I went up and spoke to Noel's coach, Santosh, who was on-duty as part of the event organising team, helping and coordinating with the participants. He said calmly, 'Sir, the only way we can get Noel to focus is to make a dramatic change in our approach.' I asked impatiently, 'What exactly has to be done, Santosh? We have to get him in the pool and get him to focus!'

He then came up with a surprising action plan.

'Please procure permission from the head of the organising committee of the event to allow me to swim alongside Noel in the adjacent lane, so that the boy can be charged up and he can follow me. He will be compelled to focus if I am in the next lane. The director will give it due consideration if it comes from a parent. The boy is severely handicapped in this kind of set-up and he needs help.'

The head of the event was a swimming champion of yesteryears, whom I had heard of in my school days. She was at the venue, surrounded by various officials. I cleaved a path through the officials and told her about the situation with Noel. I explained to her that handicaps in autism need out-of-the-box crutches. 'It is only to give them a level playing field,' I said.

Her first reaction has remained etched in my mind. She said, 'The fact that Noel, despite all his deficiencies, has come all the way from Delhi to Mumbai to take part and that he made it to the second round should be considered good enough. You should be satisfied with that. You should celebrate that.'

I replied calmly, 'But when you know that he can do much better with support, then why should we deny him that? And why should we all give up so easily? It will surprise you to see what he can do. We must not give up so easily.'

She heard me out but refused. I walked away. I sat down next to Noel, who was in his swimming trunks with a white robe wrapped around him, still ranting, 'Space ... space!' I closed my eyes as I began to reconcile myself to the fact that we had come to a dead end at the event. I was preparing myself to buy tickets and leave by the last flight that night. Just then, there was a tap on my shoulder.

It was the event director. 'If you are sure this will work as a way of support for the boy, then please go ahead and ask his coach to get ready.' She'd had a change of heart!

Santosh swiftly changed from his formal attire into his trunks, came up to the distraught boy and said in a firm, rational tone, 'Noel, we will swim together. You will follow me. Won't you?'

Noel, with tears still rolling down his eyes, looked at Santosh for one whole minute and then a crestfallen 'Yes' followed. I was excited. We were back in the game! However, nobody could predict if Santosh's strategy would work. As Noel and Santosh settled into their respective lanes, I watched all the people in the crowd gradually turning to look at Noel. Everyone had one question on their mind: 'Can the boy do it?' Nobody was wondering whether he would qualify. They only wanted to see him swim the length.

I wanted more. I wanted him to qualify for both the finals— the 25-meter freestyle and backstroke events. If he made the timing mark, he would qualify. As the whistle blew, I saw a miracle unfold. Santosh was shouting hysterically, 'Stop whining! You can do it. Come on, Noel, swim fast. Go as fast as a car!' Santosh swam ahead with a burst of energy and for a moment, Noel, distracted, stood still. But suddenly, his focus returned after watching his coach and listening to the screams from the poolside, cheering him on. He was the last in the row to start. Noel swam as fast as he could and, incredibly, overtook all other swimmers even though they had had a big lead. He had beaten all estimations of time! I was in a state of disbelief. What I saw that day, I shall remember all my life: the amazing influence and motivating powers of a coach. The nature of that relationship is so difficult to define. It was a moment when I felt that Noel had been touched by God.

The people who had been watching the complex struggle between father, son and coach gave Noel a standing ovation, one that came from the bottom of their hearts. Seeing hundreds of people on their feet applauding my son brought tears of joy to my eyes. There is something so beautiful to see compassion and human emotions expressed so spontaneously.

It was as if all the barriers broke for Noel that day. He was in the final race for both events—freestyle and backstroke. The next morning, we started early. Noel was in a comparatively settled state, but the challenge was to go back to the first venue, a smaller and noisier area with a snack counter near the pool. On the positive side, the venue would no longer be totally new for the boy. Noel had become quite popular with everyone and was greeted warmly by one and all. The previous day's dramatic finish gave him instant recognition. The boy did not have any understanding of winning a competition or defeating any other person. He just knew that in the end, it was good to get a medal because it would make his Baba, Mum and his coach happy and proud. There was no sense of personal accomplishment for him, no inner sense of triumph.

The final race began. Yet again, I had made my request to the director early in the day to retain the same 'crutch' for Noel so that he could focus. My request was accepted at once. The director had bought into my argument about fairness after the previous day's dramatic, unexpected outcome. Everybody understood that being able to focus and cutting through the anxieties that clamped Noel was key to showing his natural talent. There was his disability in play and he needed his 'crutch' to compete on a level playing field. Santosh moved into the unoccupied last lane alongside the one assigned to Noel. He looked at the boy and said once again, 'Noel, you can do it, you're a good swimmer. Keep looking at me. Just do what I have taught you. Move fast like a car!'

It was yet another miraculous performance in the freestyle race by Noel. He clocked a good time and was placed second. Shortly after that, the back-stroke event started and this time, Santosh did not have to get into the pool anymore. Noel was focused and charged up. The 'space … space' stim had disappeared. He understood the start signal better now. He was confident. He swam well and won the gold!

The award ceremony took place by the poolside. There was an enormous crowd. Noel received applause as he went up on the victory stand two times. However, Noel himself showed no expression of jubilation. In minutes, the after-effects of the swimming competition had evaporated from Noel's mind as we got into a cab. He was now only interested in listening to his Abba Gold CD. He politely asked the cab driver if he could listen to it on the car's music system. The cabbie obliged and Noel was very pleased.

Unlike Noel, I was still thinking about the high drama of the competition and all the ups and downs that we had gone through in the past few days. I was emotionally drained. I looked at him and my mind was filled with the realisation that Noel had never felt any pressure to win and get ahead of others. In this fiercely competitive world, I wondered if that should be counted as a blessing.

———

'I do not want to do this!' was often Noel's emphatic refusal.

He did not want me to nag or yak at him all the time.

This was a new insight. Noel had moved into his twenties and direct instructions or commands were not acceptable to the young man anymore. Age appropriateness is a complicated thing on the spectrum. In some areas, it plays up and in others, the notion appears irrelevant.

I had to make a change in approach to register compliance. I had to uncover a new key to charge him up. With that as the backdrop, one day, Noel and I were on the cyclist's path in Lodhi Gardens. At the end of the lane, I asked, 'Can you move forward to the end of the lane and then make a U-turn? Can you do this alone?' The gentle question had the desired effect.

'I can do this alone, Baba,' was his reassuring response.

CHAPTER SEVEN

My Gifted Golf Teacher

There was a strong wind blowing. It was a hot summer morning in Kolkata. But the quiet and the magnificence of the sylvan green had enveloped me in a cheerful state of mind. The splendour of the club's golf course was pure delight to the eyes and somehow relegated the discomfort of the heat to the background—it did not seem to matter. I sat in the shade under a tree near the golf practice area where ten-year-old Noel was having a session with his golf instructor, Amar Singh.

That summer vacation in Kolkata proved to be an extraordinary one because Pia had introduced Noel to Amar, a golf trainer in his early forties. He said that he never had the chance to study in a school and was a man of modest means trying his best to support his small family. He was unsure how long he was going to be able to fund his son's education. Since childhood, he had spent his life on various golf courses, earning money on a daily basis. First as a ball boy, then as a caddie and, finally, as an instructor. Over the years, he had taught the upscale game of golf to many of the rich and famous, he said and one could not miss the note of irony present in his voice as he spoke.

I watched them from the vantage point under the tree as the practice session began—I had to be careful to be out of Noel's line of sight because my presence would certainly distract him. Noel was calm and a picture of concentration, complying with every word that was said by his instructor. He got into the correct stance, trying his best to get the grip right with both his hands, focusing on the right degree of swing in every shot. He went on chipping for more than half an hour. It was an unbelievable sight! Who would imagine that Noel was no regular child? That he was actually an autistic boy with difficulties of hyperactivity and obsessive behaviours, with an inability to modulate his hand grip according to the desired degree? Every time Noel executed a reasonably good shot, Amar, standing behind Noel, would turn around and wave at me excitedly, 'Did you see that?'

My mind was clouded with concerns as I closely observed the training proceedings. The first concern that had flashed through my mind was Noel's incorrigible obsession with the hard, dimpled surface of the golf ball, something he'd been obsessed with since he had been four. On almost every trip to the club, he would slink around and snatch new golf balls from the club shop. I would come to know after the bill came to me. Would he be able to restrain himself from running away with the golf ball instead of following the instructor's prompts?

The second concern that swirled in my head had to do with my apprehensions about the instructor. Was Amar trying to make a quick buck by merely passing some time with Noel? A common concern that parents of disabled children always harbour. The third concern was that would Noel be able to make any progress in a sport requiring so much eye and muscle coordination, precision and concentration?

Well, there he was, right before my eyes, looking smart in a bright yellow sports shirt and the club's golf cap, chipping away with precision. My apprehensions melted away. Amar was a gifted teacher. Gifted enough to strike a rapport with an autistic child. It did not matter to Amar how many times Noel made a mistake. While that is to be expected from any coach, Amar's innovative touch was his monologue that he kept up as Noel was taking his shots—about how great the game of golf was and how easily Noel could learn it. He talked about some history of the game and how enjoyable it would be for Noel to play on the course once he had learnt it. He kept up a gentle, natural, conversational tone while helping Noel get his grip on the putter. I realised the potential power of the right tone of voice in a teaching situation for a neurodivergent child as I watched this incredibly talented teacher. It did not matter to him whether Noel comprehended his continuous commentary. The real insight that flashed through my mind was that Amar was able to gradually uncover Noel's desire to do something right. Lack of motivation is in itself a disability of the intellect and it is very hard for most people to grasp that. Amar appeared to have a gut feeling about this sort of thing.

There was no impatience and no molly-coddling either. But there was undiluted elation when Noel executed a good shot. Noel felt wonderfully and unconditionally accepted by Amar. And this was the golden key. He knew that his teacher respected him and his differences. Noel felt that Amar understood his inability to get things right even when he was genuinely trying hard. His coach did not bring upon him any performance anxiety whatsoever. Noel knew he had the freedom, yet he felt good that Amar was in control. This was useful, since I was also just getting familiar with the challenges of raising Noel and was keenly observant of what worked or didn't work. I have to say, in reflection, that this 'control' aspect is indeed a complex perceptional balance to arrive at. The autistic child's mind generally holds a psychological craving for control over their immediate environment, which often manifests in problematic behaviours.

I noticed that Noel liked to hold Amar's arm when they walked about in the club. It signified very high comfort levels and his trust in the man. The next few days that I was in Kolkata, I went every morning to watch the practice sessions. It was a real joy for me to see Noel make rapid progress. Amar told me that he would procure second-hand golf clubs for Noel so that he could continue his training in Delhi after the vacation. And he said something that I will never forget as he bid me farewell.

'Noel is God's special gift to all of us. All of us have to treat him with kindness, care and respect. Anybody who hurts him has to be an idiot! He would face the wrath of God! Believe me, being with him has changed me—there is so much beauty in his innocence.'

He shook my hand, turned to leave, then halted. 'Sir, in Noel's case,' said Amar in a serious tone, 'Please don't depend only on doctors. Through kindness, love and faith, we can bring a lot of change in him.'

Respect, tolerance and kindness for the disabled are indicative of a higher state of being, and developing such characteristics early is important. Parents must put that on their agenda. Let's not leave this to the schools to take up and induct such values in the child. It must begin at home.

Our enthusiasm in getting Noel to step up his swimming skills, and our painstaking efforts in working with him in other sporting activities—tennis, golf, swimming, cycling, walking, roller skating, squash—was beginning to show results on several fronts, particularly, muscle building, stamina enhancement, enhanced sensory integration and better motor skills. That's when I got to know about Daily Living Therapy (DLT), a method of education for children on the autism spectrum, an idea that was developed by Dr Kiyo Kitahara, the founder of the renowned Musashino Higashi School in Tokyo (set up in 1987). Vigorous physical activities and group sporting activities are foundational to this method. My belief that a strong and intensive physical activity regime would bring dividends was now solidly reinforced as I started to read more and more about this method and its multi-faceted dimensions (You can read an outline about DLT reproduced from the MHS website in Appendix Two).

In 2003, a lucky coincidence occurred. As I was reading about DLT on the internet, I got a surprise call from my client to visit Tokyo—I was required to attend an international marketing summit. It was to be my first trip to Japan! I was excited as this would mean I would be able to work out a way to visit Musashino Higashi Junior School facilities, including the MHS Vocational High School, a separate unit that focuses on vocational training!

I spent considerable time at the latter school block absorbing everything around me. The relevance of a vocational training system was in no way relevant at that time for Noel, but my innate interest lay in this area. The noticeable features of the complex were the jogging track and the basketball court, both indoors. These were not merely facilities for sports, but used frequently by the students in their late teens and their early youth as mechanisms to diffuse anxiety and stress. It was indeed very thoughtfully designed. Then there was a large cafeteria where autistic youngsters learnt kitchen work, catering, baking, accounts and bank work and so on; the sub-activities were tailored to each individual's interest. The well-known Japanese hospitality was simply enthralling. The institution had pre-arranged everything, including an MHS executive who was an excellent English-Japanese interpreter. The head of the school had put me on his meeting schedule for the day, he walked me through the history and provided a quick understanding of the MHS schools, including the one in Massachusets, USA (Boston Higashi School) and the DLT method, and how it gets autistic individuals ready for employment in the real world. I had the privilege of interacting with the educators and instructors in the vocational block; they appeared to be deeply committed to the continuous development of the young people there.

Looking back, all of these experiences had given me lifelong learnings that moulded my worldview about autism, sporting activities and the vocational training space.

———

Noel, fourteen, was posed with the question 'Can you tell me what are the things a gentleman will always do?'

The boy was by then familiar with the notion of a 'gentleman' owing to repetitive whisper prompts: 'Always be a gentleman, Noel.'

So, he knew it was hard, but it was the gentleman's way that was praised and liked. Noel verbally listed his choices, with a slight pause after every point, while I kept count, extending my thumb first and then the other fingers, one by one.

'A gentleman drinks coffee, helps others, never shouts, waits for his turn and plays golf. Baba, I am a gentleman!'

———

One Sunday evening, we were hanging around in the putting practice area at Siri Fort for a refreshing break.

What elevated my spirits was watching Noel swing his putter flawlessly and his ability to push aside the surge of distractions that we don't even notice for a second in the usual course of things. The swirl of birds just above the putting area, the powerful lights in the corners, a bawling baby in the adjacent café, and suddenly, an airplane passing by with a piercing boom—all these were so difficult to block for Noel owing to his oversensitivity. In spite of all that, he continued to strive hard to concentrate and improve his putting.

CHAPTER EIGHT

Where is the Room in the Mushroom?

'Baba, Noel's jacket is wet!' Noel, eight, announced this with a certain urgency as he sat in the front seat of the car. It was a sunny winter morning, I remember. I thought he had perhaps spilt water while drinking, which might be causing discomfort to his oversensitive skin. I stopped the car and checked him carefully. There was no sign of wetness. Then, for a moment, I thought it might be a post-toilet situation. I checked for that as well but found nothing to be damp.

'No, your jacket is not wet,' I said, puzzled. The boy whined insistently, 'Baba, it is wet!' A thought struck me. Noel was actually feeling warm and wanted to remove his jacket.

Noel's verbal cue to ask for his clothes to be changed was simply: 'Clothes are wet.' His takeaway from past experience was that if he was uncomfortable and wanted to change or remove his clothes, all he had to say was, 'Noel's shirt is wet! Trousers are wet!' and so on. Right at that moment, the real discomfort was that he was feeling very warm in the jacket.

This is an example of the issue of contextual interpretation in Noel's mind. This points us to the serious challenges that children with autism have to navigate with language constructs and labelling. To wear the left shoe on the left foot and the right shoe on the right is perhaps a reflex action that we never even pause to think about, even as small children. Once you know it, you never go wrong for the rest of your life. However, for the autistic mind, it can be a monumental task to get it correct and then to get it correct all the time! Suddenly, you realise what you take for granted has to be taught with extreme care and precision to someone because of the different way in which they process information. The nuance of the shoe shape that is obvious to us was often overlooked by Noel.

For Noel, a shoe was to be worn on the foot. The differentiation of the left shoe and the right would be, for him, an unnecessary detail. Even if it is wrong to wear the right shoe on the left foot, why bother with this incorrectness? This was the unspoken thought. We had to accept that point of view rather than insist on ours. This was a lesson for Pia and me. This mode of generalising was clearly an innate defensive trait. It was necessary, perhaps, to cut down on the details beyond a point for his unique processing system. Over time, he learnt to follow the shoe shape, but he needed us to prompt him with a 'Check!' with the finger pointing at his shoes.

Over time, we also understood that for Noel, words were

labels that encoded several associated things or people; he bunched them together mentally. For instance, once he had understood the name 'Romit' belonged to his cousin, he would expect people who resembled Romit in appearance to respond to the name Romit as well. This led to many an amusing situation, especially when we were travelling with Noel and he would find co-passengers resembling a relative of ours or a close family friend and expect them to be cordial towards him. He would begin to follow them around. The question 'What is in a name?' had unusual connotations in Noel's mind. According to him, anything that smelled like a rose and looked somewhat like a rose must also be called a rose.

Noel's labelling of various feelings was somewhat like putting together a mismatched jigsaw, with the pieces coming together from different puzzles. It was confounding for his caregivers. Once in the middle of a peaceful Sunday afternoon, Noel, then fifteen, declared that he was getting a heart attack! I kept my calm and asked, 'Noel, what is the reason?'

This was a question to which he had started to respond verbally (in English mainly and, to an extent, in Bengali and Hindi). His response had to be extracted carefully by encouraging him to thread his lines of logic. Caution had to be applied in a balanced manner so that it did not overwhelm the child.

Part of my home-teaching strategy through his teens had been to stabilise his thoughts, induce him to reflect inwardly, prompt thought-starters, point to tangible reason as far as possible or get him to choose from multiple answers, all the while engaging him verbally.

What is the reason? This innocuous question became for me a useful tool. The answers did not come in the initial stages. Noel took a couple of years of training to process and relate to this question flawlessly. Perhaps for many children on the autism spectrum, this question sits at the base of the myriad potential opportunities for learning. I would advocate this approach strongly especially when you are looking at behaviour modification.

Noel's solemn response that Sunday afternoon was, 'Baba, I had many masala dosas for breakfast. That is why I am getting a heart attack!'

I leapt at the opportunity to help the boy navigate the oddities of the English language.

'Noel, that is not a heart attack. It is called heartburn,'

This stupefied Noel. 'But Baba, we didn't start the fire.'

After a mental tussle, I understood. He was recalling Billy Joel's song. Song lyrics helped him to express himself. Often, this resulted in hotch-potch segments of verbal communication, but if you could make allowances for zany associations, then life was good.

His line of reasoning: burns happen when there is a fire and with the masala dosas, there was no fire, so nothing got burnt. We all quote song lyrics now and then in daily conversation, but with Noel, it was different. There was no deliberate twist, sarcasm, embellishment or cleverness in quoting any lines. For him, it was a simple substitute for basic, functional communication. On a separate register, his innocence made it even more charming to most of us.

Noel had an abundance of lyrics in his repertoire that were applicable across different clusters of contexts. The answer was always embedded in that fragment of lyric that he had picked for the situation. Using such lyrics with signifiers had become a survival skill that he had honed. It worked and became a robust technique over time. His mother, sister and I constantly encouraged him to do so, although we could not hold back the inevitable chuckle that this nuanced and inventive method of communication would invoke in us.

Unfortunately, the English language can be complex to navigate, even after you have successfully taught someone how to respond to 'How are you feeling?' or 'What is the reason the job was not done?' There is that struggle with words that sound similar, i.e., right/write, sea/see, hear/here, brake/break and then there are words such as 'watch', which can mean two different things, even though it's spelt the same way. The maze of homophonic words, similar or different spellings, brought on many unanticipated hurdles. Noel was always an audio-based learner. The problem of homophones compounded across the other two languages in everyday use as well—Hindi and Bengali.

At a restaurant, Noel's first query, at six years of age when a bowl of mushroom soup arrived on his table, was, 'Baba, where *is* the room in the mushroom?' This remained unresolved in his mind for the rest of his life. That question invariably popped up whenever 'mushroom' was mentioned—'There's room in a living room, bedroom, bathroom. Is there a room inside the mushroom?'

The word *cheel* in Bengali is the word for kite, the bird. There was one that would sometimes appear, swooping solo, in the area we lived in. Noel learnt from our Bengali housemaid that the big dark bird is a *cheel*. Noel was quite scared when the kite stopped by on our fourth-floor balcony next to his room and he would run into the inner bedrooms whenever he sighted her staring at him.

There is a very popular restaurant called The Big Chill in the neighbourhood. So, for Noel, the nuance of the pronunciation of 'chill' and '*cheel*' was negligible. In his view, the restaurant's name stood for The Big Kite, The Big *Cheel*. What solidified his presumption was that on the walls of the trendy retro decor of The Big Chill hung a framed poster of Alfred Hitchcock's classic, *The Birds*. Noel always avoided sitting at the table next to that scary poster. To him, it was his nemesis, the *cheel*! It was an interesting development since Noel had acquired the ability to simultaneously balance two contradictory emotions. In my book, this was a sign of emotional growth, a leap forward. He clearly did not approve of the name of the restaurant because of its associations with an object of fear, but was willing to make allowances as he enjoyed the cuisine and ambience of the eatery. It remained his favourite restaurant, even with that scary poster inside.

On top of this, Noel had a tendency to craft labels with a certain generalisation, usually resulting in a mishmash. For example, looking at a tiny mechanical metal spring (that had come out of a broken toy car) and sitting in a far-away spot, Noel would giggle, 'Baba, there is a spring lying there without a chicken!' Voila! The fried spring chicken that was on the restaurant menu was the culprit for this mumbo-jumbo. There is no formal training course that Pia or I could have taken to become good at cracking Noel's code of labelling.

Noel would talk of Amlan Sir, a teacher to whom he had been very attached. Amlan Sir had moved to Canada and there was no regular contact with him. The last time he spoke to Noel was on the phone when he had visited Delhi. On a walk in the evening, Noel declared, 'Amlan Sir is not in the world anymore.' Astounded, I looked at him and said, 'Noel, you know he is in Canada and Canada is in this world.'

Pat came the answer, 'Canada is out of this world!' I was befuddled. He had obviously heard someone use the idiom to describe the beauty of a place. His interpretation was surreal. Idioms could play havoc for Noel. Imagine how a metaphorical expression such as, 'Now you can dance your heart out', would be processed by him!

Another language-related aspect is self-learning through observation and then there was his quirky take on the use of the various short phrases in everyday conversation. When Noel heard me use the line, 'I don't feel like driving today,' on the phone, he became visibly excited at the thought of having discovered a legitimate excuse. I remember the glint in his eyes when he heard me say that and the relish with which he echoed it several times after.

One evening, he strategically unleashed it. On our way back from the usual cycling drill, Noel, then seventeen, wanted a Cola from the market roadside shop. I halted the car a bit away from the shop, owing to congestion in the area, handed him a Rs 500 note and asked him to buy his drink. It was an act he could handle independently at this point.

Noel returned with his soda, and settled into the car's back seat instead of the front so that he could stretch his legs and enjoy his drink.

'Give me the balance money, Noel?'

'Baba, I did not feel like collecting the balance.'

'Noel, you must collect the balance from the shopkeeper ... always! Please go back. It is Rs 460!'

'Well, I don't feel like it!'

Another recount from his early school days to illustrate the linguistic hurdles for the autistic child and the caregiver strikes me at this moment.

'Can I have a horse burger for my tiffin tomorrow?'

Bizarre? Yes, absolutely! Noel went back to toying with the calculator. I gave it a pass. However, the thought simply did not leave my head.

After a while, I decoded the answer. Noel would have a fillet burger, shorthand for 'fillet of fish burger', packed for his tiffin occasionally. He had not been told what exactly a fillet meant. No one had bothered to tell him. Its' articulation resembles the word 'filly' phonetically. Noel was familiar with the horse, the mare and the filly thanks to educational games on the iPad. Thus, if he could have filly meat in his burger, why not the meat of an adult horse?

The stumbles of vocabulary and expressive speech continued as Noel approached twenty. Profuse interjections of echolalia remained; it was an unending web of single words coupled with short and long sentences, repeating exactly what had been spoken by the other person.

In parallel, teaching him the concept of 'self-referencing' in verbal expressions had been a steady challenge, but there had been improvements through repeated prompts in everyday situations. The self-referencing, the understanding of the self as an entity and that it had to be communicated using language in the first person was arduous. To make legible the abstractness of 'me, my, I' appeared to be a Herculean task. I would repeatedly mention this by speaking to him and pointing at him with my index finger. Then I would follow up by actually touching his chest with my finger. This tangible physical action helped to reinforce the understanding somewhat. In his mind, the whole sense of a self gradually started to get established and even enter his speech. 'I' and 'Noel' intermingled, i.e., 'Noel will also travel,' or 'I like to sit here,' or 'Noel saw a bench in the park,' or 'Noel is feeling sad.'

There is an episode in self-referencing that has remained a distinct memory. We were at the reception of a reputed vocational institution in Delhi. Noel, eighteen, was called into the admission office for a face-to-face interview accompanied by me. The first question the headmistress asked was, 'What is your name, young man?' Silence filled the air and all eyes were on the lanky lad. Looking up at her, he said, 'My name is Khan ... I am a gentleman,' and extended his arm to shake hands.

I groaned internally. If you have watched the Bollywood movie by that name, then you can catch the reference. Noel had recently seen the Shah Rukh Khan blockbuster. He had repeatedly been told that he was like Shah Rukh Khan, the protagonist, a young man with Asperger's. The gracious lady was naturally perplexed by this. It made little sense to her, nor did she find it funny. It was very awkward for me as I tried to mumble an explanation. Such unexpected bumps in social interchanges were a regular part of our lives.

Noel hit a home run on this track of self-referencing when he woke me up one night around 2.30 a.m., saying 'Baba, please chat with me!' This he followed with the perfect Bengali version of the same sentence: 'Baba, *amar saathey golpo korbey.*' My reaction, I must confess, was one of irritation at being woken up before it dawned on me that this was the perfect usage of the first person—a self-identity construct and that too in two distinct languages. It was a victorious moment!

This trajectory of self-referencing—the formation of self-identity grew in leaps and bounds. When a friend told him, 'Hey Noel, you are a good-looker, like Gregory Peck!' or when Ahvana insisted, 'You look just like Peter Pan,' Noel would get visibly irked. 'Nah! I am Noel Paul. Nothing else.' The message was: This rock of identity cannot be shifted; look-alike compliments, social nuances and niceties were clearly not okay!

Returning to my question of, 'What is the reason?', drawing from the fountainhead of structure and embedding it in the question is a cause-effect tool that can be used effectively as a teaching strategy, which I have underlined. Its success entailed considerable investment in time and patience. His responses had to be carefully prodded to overcome the repetitions, guiding him to completion.

One idea that stemmed from teaching through catalysing thoughts was to ask Noel to define things and place them visually in a very simple structure, using fingers as a visual aid or numbering them in ascending order.

I also worked valiantly to prevent Noel from hearing any swear words so that he didn't add them to his inventory of new words or use them in social situations, such as at the swimming pool or at school. Even if unintended, such words could very well have appeared in his echolalic speech and caused profound embarrassment. I had to constantly distract him as soon as I caught someone in his presence using foul language, including the ever-present 'F' word and other frequently heard Hindi or Bengali abuses. The telling evidence of the success of this initiative has been Noel's oft-used expression of maximum disgust in a terse tone: 'Damn, damn!' If an autorickshaw suddenly appeared in front of our car in the middle of a crowded market lane, causing it to screech to a sudden halt, you could expect him to immediately yelp his signature 'Damn, damn.' It's possible to say that this characteristic feature of 'no abusive language ever' was another gentlemanly thing in his repertoire!

———

In winter, our security guard often greeted Noel with, 'Toh Noel ji, aaj kal kya chal raha hai? (So, Noel, what's going on these days).' Instead, of the customary, 'Sab thik chal raha hai, (Everything is going okay)' answer, the boy would take the question beyond a greeting and sincerely reply, 'Heater! Heater chal raha hai. (The heater is 'going' on nowadays).'

Noel used to draw the heater really close to him and crouch like a cat. Irked by his overuse of the heater, I would holler that the electricity bill will hit us badly. Noel's instant reaction would be to place the heater about five feet away and settling down again, ask in utter earnestness, 'Will this make the bill amount less?'

In another manifestation of electricity bill blues, he once insisted our driver stop switching on the car lights, reminding him rather assertively to cut down on the power consumption so that the bill was not too high for his dad.

———

In his bid to join conversations at the breakfast table, Noel would seek entry points and he figured if any words surfaced that he was familiar with, he would move in by stringing the word with something. He did not always quite comprehend the context, but his urge for social communication had risen in his late teens.

His abrupt entries were always amusing. Here is an instance. As I looked through the newspaper, I announced loudly for the benefit of all around the breakfast table that the Delhi Chief Minister, Arvind Kejriwal, would be imposing an odd-even scheme for private cars in a bid to check pollution. There was a hint of a mild threat in my tone, I guess, because Noel jumped in with, 'Baba, no odd behaviour, Kejriwal is strict.'

———

One morning, as part of my regular question time, I asked Noel, 'Hey Noel, what is the name of the boss of YouTube? Come on, quick?' I was pointing at the famous Google CEO's picture on my phone. Noel answered with a big grin, 'Sundar dikhtaa hai!'

———

'Noel, your mom, just messaged me, she has just reached Lisbon for that international conference! Any message from you that you want me to pass on to her?' I asked.

'Confidence for conference!' came his rather loud cheery reply.

Noel's fascination for similar sounding words and their spontaneous use was everyday entertainment!

———

We generally used to saunter around in the Alakananda market, South Delhi on Sunday evenings. Once, Noel walked up to check the tawa of a tikkiwala, temptation was written all over his face. I put on my stern face tone and said, 'Noel, tikkis are very oily ... not allowed. Let's go!'

Noel bent over, studied the sizzling tikkis floating teasingly in the abundance of bubbling cheap oil and remarked, 'Baba, they are not oily, they are looking happy!'

CHAPTER NINE

I Will Never Make You Sad

An important milestone had arrived. Noel had turned sixteen. The preceding years of adolescence had been a mixed bag. On the one hand, some big strides in functional learning had been achieved at school and on the other, some complex behavioural challenges had caused us frustration and helplessness.

However, our strategy to mould learning according to Noel's preferences and pace continued at home and at school. While Noel certainly occupied nearly 90 per cent of our minds, our careers still needed to be navigated and occupational commitments had to be met. We could not afford any derailment there, despite the heavy demands on our time, our juggling of work and having to be hands-on with Noel at home was mandatory. Personal finances, our social and extended family commitments, our ageing parents and their health issues, office politics and Ahvana's academics had to be handled with equanimity and poise using the remaining 10 per cent of our available mental energy. I had mastered living this unusual life.

At sixteen, Noel stood six feet in height and was a strong bloke. He was a swimming star in his own right with exceptional strength in his limbs. In contrast, his face was soft and sweet, his eyes full of innocence, always radiating kindness. His infectious 1000-watt grin that invariably coaxed a smile onto others' faces had remained unchanged. His instant and intense empathy for others had only grown as he turned older.

When he saw children come up to the car window at the red light, begging for money, he appeared to be filled with confusion and sympathy. 'Baba, I want to take the poor kid home. He can have a bath. He can have some food. I will sing songs with him. Baba, please let's take him home.' It was difficult to reason with him why that wasn't possible.

He was still trying to figure out the world around him and he had his usual bag of mischievous and attention-seeking tactics well in tow. While there was plenty of independent, self-initiated, meaningful speech, there was still a surfeit of echolalia speech and repetitive self-talk. He had now been coached in various daily chores around the kitchen. Our expression was always, 'Noel will now help,' in a gentle tone. We made it a point to never encode the request with any visible pressure, whether it was chopping vegetables, laying the dinner table, filling the water jug and so on. Our strategy flowed from this concept of boosting self-worth through the process of helping with housework and in that, leveraging the particular strengths of the child. To ask for help with the option of refusal, without any pressure, was the key to easy compliance and one that made the task particularly satisfying for him.

Noel had a very short span of attention for desk-bound rote-learning tasks and one-on-one teaching sessions. The conventional teaching method of sitting across the table had limited returns. He would get bored rather quickly by the monotonous two-way method of pedagogy. It was the same in school. Also implicit in that set-up was the pressure of a teacher looking over the learner's work, which discomfited Noel as conveyed by his body language. Acute pressure would get him so flustered that he would start to spit on the study table. The first reaction for me or the teacher would be to reprimand the boy then and there. But upon reflection, I understood that the educator, whoever wore that hat, even with a controlled tonality, would get the boy to feel inadequate by the admonishment of his spitting. The across-the-table method looked easy when I would watch the TEACCH* training videotapes, but they didn't work for Noel. Though I hasten to add that the core idea of TEAACH of structure-sequence no-distractions technique was very useful in the early stages and I shared the video training modules with Noel's educators at the school, too.

---

*TEACCH is the acronym for Treatment & Education of Autistic & Related Communication Handicapped Children, a clinical, training and research program based at the University of North Carolina, Chapel Hill, USA. The TEACCH programme uses a method for teaching functional academics and then progresses to higher levels, including vocational training. It's founded on the application of various aids (mostly visual) in the classroom or workspace environment which is highly structured and sequential to help students on the autism spectrum learn and perform.

Years rolled by and Noel was not making much progress in school in functional academics, which was worrisome because he was already bang in the middle of adolescence. He gained a lot in school through everything outside of academic learning. How strange that must sound! However, he had developed a strong emotional bond with his teachers, whom he considered his friends. His communication skills started to develop and accelerate. He loved to go for walks on the school field with his teachers and break into prolonged monologues without the fear of being pulled up, as no assertive disciplining was ever applied. That was truly positive and helped Noel's self-confidence blossom.

His passion for cars, transportation as a general theme, music and food—the well-recognised strands of narrow, rigid and obsessive interests, classical characteristics of autism remained unchanged as he entered his sixteenth year. His communication skills in terms of intent and comprehension had moved forward, though he could not read or write beyond some elementary copying. By then he could answer rather well, as a result of home teaching, to questions such as 'Why are you doing this?' or 'What is the reason this has happened?'

However, he still had a massive block when it came to communicating his frustrations and fears or even fundamental needs. He would resort to hollering, oblivious of where he was and who was around him. The triggers were not always possible to fathom, but one trigger that we understood was hunger. The other was loneliness. There were several others that we were still clueless about.

It was always on my mind that Noel's inability to communicate with his closest buddies—his father and mother—about his apprehensions, frustrations and his sense of inadequacy must have caused excruciating mental agony in that phase of puberty. The confusion over his bodily changes and the frightening, unfathomable yet pleasurable aspects of sexual arousal were only some of the many sparks that ignited Noel's insecure feelings. His sudden aggressive outbursts were perhaps linked to feelings of guilt and led to self-hate owing to the havoc his body was causing. He must have felt imprisoned by his corporeality.

The frequent destruction of decorative artefacts, crystals and so on that was plucked out of our living room décor was incessant. During that stormy period, on one occasion when Pia and Ahvana were travelling outstation, I was alone with Noel for a week. One evening, I had to step out for a pressing official engagement and left Noel alone at home. I could not arrange for any help to keep watch on the boy while I was going to be away. Noel was somewhat displeased about my leaving him alone, but finally came around when I promised I would be back in two hours. Noel was still not clear about the abstract notions of the quantum of time. However, he knew that two hours wasn't very long. Typically, he would look at pictorial books and magazines or listen to music on his tape recorder. He always had his favourite audio music cassettes handy so that he would be comfortable on his own.

I had a fruitful meeting and was relieved when I wrapped up and arrived at the door exactly in two hours. It was around 10 p.m. and as I unlocked the main door to our flat, I suddenly had a sense of foreboding that something had gone awry. So, I stepped forward, quite tensed, into the dark hallway. All of a sudden, I realised that I was walking on fine pieces of broken objects. I switched on the living room lights. There was a tsunami of sorts, an upheaval! You could say that I was standing in the middle of a crime scene and felt a slight queasiness rising in my gut. I gathered my composure and waded through broken plates, cups and bowls that crowded the floors. There was not a square inch of space that was not covered with broken pieces of porcelain or glass.

I panicked, expecting to see a bleeding and badly injured Noel as I tiptoed across the dining area and then to his bedroom. There he was on the floor! He looked up at me with a wicked grin. Although he was sitting right in the middle of infinite pieces of broken glass, Noel was safe! I heaved a sigh of relief. It was like suffering death and then scrambling back to life. As I thanked the cosmic forces for saving Noel from injury, I realised it had been a big mistake to leave him alone. The gnawing clutch of guilt made me sick.

I was calm. I did not scold him. In fact, I did not say a word to the boy. It was clear from his facial expressions that he had been expecting an angry reaction; a much-longed-for hoopla that would add to his thrill. I figured out what had happened. All the dinner sets and all the crockery had been pulled out from the large sideboard that had mistakenly been left unlocked in the dining area and they had been smashed into pieces one by one by the protesting soul. I poured a small drink to calm my nerves and settled into a chair.

The monetary loss was considerable, but what hurt even more was the loss of some valued lifetime possessions. They were treasured wedding gifts that we had received from our close friends and relatives. Every home has a special place for such articles and they had come to be used and shown around at family get-togethers and celebrations and were equivalents of heirlooms, preserved with much sentiment and pride. All these thoughts were quickly relegated to the background, as the question that swirled in my head was: why did Noel do this? What had triggered this destructive display of frustration? Was it actually about registering his protest, which I had presumed in my first reaction? Was this the mode of communication that he had been compelled to resort to in the face of suppressed anger?

I sat him down. I was very calm. I told him flatly, slowly, in a few words, that this was not acceptable; I told him that this had hurt me and I was feeling very sad. If he was upset, then he must talk to me and not break things. Noel was pensive. He left the room without a word. In about fifteen minutes, he came back to me and said, 'Baba, I will break nothing. I will never make you sad.' Thereafter, at regular intervals, he would come up to me and plead with me, repeating the same words in a sorrowful tone. He was feeling extremely guilty. I knew I should assuage his guilt at that very moment. Often, I had noticed if it was not actively brought down, it led to hyperactivity and that would in turn blow into a meltdown, possibly leading to self-injury. It had to be extinguished then and there. So, I put my arm around his shoulder warmly and said, 'It's alright, I know you are sad; I am also sad. But everything will become okay. Got it?' Noel's teary reply was, 'Got it, Baba.'

Guilt with Noel had to be handled with kid gloves. This remained a non-negotiable principle. There was self-teaching here that parents must be constantly open to, I have to say. A lesson had to be imbibed in those situations. Re-occurrences had to be proactively prevented. Any reinforcement had to be sustained, yet caution had to be exercised not to push him over the threshold of guilt where he lost all his emotional control, causing his rage to become self-directed. Something commonly known is that guilt and shame are self-conscious emotions. The usual observations autism researchers make about ASD children and adults is that they are usually less prone to guilt. If that is so, then I have to say Noel was an exception. He displayed an acute consciousness of guilt. Neither Noel's mum nor I could ignore the profound effect guilt had on the boy after an incident like this. We had learnt by then that guilt is the most difficult-to-understand emotion. It has strong subconscious components, unlike many other emotional states, and remains potent for extended periods of time, long after the occurrence of the episode.

So, I devised a method to convey in a very simple way what is it that I do when I feel guilty—I couldn't use the word guilty with Noel; it was too abstract for him. One had to use words that were associated with, or shall we say, representative of something he could clearly comprehend. The words I chose were 'angry' and 'impatient' and I further suggested the idea of a range of lines, like a meter, depending on the severity of the emotion that he could use to respond to the question, 'How angry are you with yourself?' Based on what he was feeling, he could read aloud one of the following lines from a card:

'I am angry with myself, but I can control myself now.'

'I am angry and impatient, but I can control myself, give me ten minutes.'

'I cannot control myself. I want a glass of nimbu paani.'

I will now recount another episode that elucidates the myriad effects of a state of guilt and the accompanying trauma this had on Noel.

It was May 2005. Pia was scheduled to leave for Sweden along with the University team. Noel had a routine schedule of special school, swimming lessons, tennis (wall practice) and weekend evening outings—I would accompany him in his activities after school. But life was not all that regulated. There were also intermittent outbursts of aggression during those teen years with no apparent cause or trigger. Head-banging, crying, shouting, pushing people who came near him to console him or pulling their shirts and so forth. Fortunately, the spurts of angst were short and he could recover rather quickly.

On the eve of her departure, Pia wanted to bake something that was Noel's all-time favourite. She chose to make lasagne, a dish she had mastered. Noel had loved eating her lasagne since he'd been a kid. It was always a grand, celebratory occasion for Noel when it was placed on the dining table in a glass casserole. He, however, appeared a bit unsettled that evening. I could sense it, but could not fathom exactly what was bothering him. Owing to her work, Pia would travel often, so that was not a new situation. I consoled myself that on Noel's sighting of the baked dish, his mood would surely change for the better.

As Pia announced dinner, Noel rushed to the kitchen and

extracted the casserole from the oven very carefully. The aroma of the dish filled the room. All of a sudden, I saw Noel's face contort and, in an inexplicable burst of anger, he raised the casserole and flung it at the floor with all his might. There was a resounding crash and the casserole was shattered. Golden-brown lasagne lay strewn on the floor, glittering with small shards of glass.

Pia broke down like never before. She had an early morning international flight and there were still many things to get done. What had gone wrong with her angelic boy? How could he destroy his favourite food when he knew his mum had made it especially for him? He'd never acted so fiercely before. Seeing his mother cry, Noel turned to jelly. He went down on his knees and pleaded over and over again, 'Sorry, sorry I will never do this again.' Pia was ballistic. 'Why Noel? Just why?' but Noel said nothing apart from begging to be forgiven by his mother.

Ten years later, it was clear that the magnitude of the trauma and the guilt associated with it appeared to have a strange grip on the boy. True to his word, he never broke anything ever again. Not in the kitchen, not in the living room, not anywhere else. In fact, a complicated part of this episode is that the shock was so great to the tender mind of the boy that he was visibly repulsed at the sight of lasagne, even in a restaurant or a bakery! He would also be filled with discomfort if he sighted anything that roughly resembled lasagne, for example, a shepherd's pie and would become nauseous at the mere suggestion of touching it. Respecting his sensitivity, his fears and the indelible sense of guilt pertaining to the subject of lasagne, we struck the Italian dish off from the culinary list at our home forever.

Guilt is not a subject that I have come across in autism literature by experts or educators. This, to my mind, is an area that must be delineated from the bundle of autistic impairments of communication, social and learning difficulties, the usual IEPs* for the child and so on. How does the autistic mind process and experience the multi-headed hydra that is guilt and how do we pull the child out of its grasp? How do we alleviate those deep-set emotions and associations? There were some definitive steps that Pia and I had formulated. Even in the face of the most mischievous or offensive act by Noel, one had to carefully calibrate the reaction. The tonality of our voice, choice of words and gestures were aspects that had to be applied judiciously. Also, there was a need to develop a sharp sense of the child's threshold to take a scolding. If you crossed that threshold, you risked inducing further guilt, resulting in another set of unacceptable behaviours, anguish or even a complete meltdown.

It was the Bengali New Year's Day, 14 April 2015. Kanchan, a stocky Bengali lady and our housemaid at the time, who was very protective and caring about Noel, had spent the whole day preparing the traditional festival special for this auspicious day: patishapta. A loose translation would be pancakes with a sweet stuffing of coconut mince.

---

*IEP is the acronym for Individualised Education Plan—special educators set the goals and methods to accomplish them within a defined time frame.

On the breakfast table, I remarked excitedly, 'They look so good!'

Noel agreed, 'Yes Baba, they look good!'

'Hey Noel, is this more exciting than burgers? What do you think?'

'Yes! Better than burgers. They are not available at McDonald's. Good job, Kanchan!'

And then suddenly there was a change in the mood. He looked at the plate disdainfully. His expression changed and he pushed the plate away. I ignored the sudden shift and said, 'Okay Noel, I am going to have one piece now and the rest will be stored in the fridge. You can have them as dessert after dinner.'

A few hours later in the office, I got a call from Pia. 'Noel has tossed the patishapta into the waste bin,' she groaned. Presumably, it resembled the fearful subject of lasagne. The colour and the texture had brought back his guilt and trauma. Despite the risk of being pulled up by his annoyed parents, Noel would take no chances with anything that looked like lasagne. Our son's obsession with his guilt related to the lasagne appeared to be insurmountable. I discussed things with Pia on that phone call and we decided to give it a quiet pass and pretended to be oblivious to what had happened.

So, life in the minefield of guilt can be a bit explosive. You have to have a strategy in place.

———

This was some years later. Noel's mother and sister were travelling, so he had been home alone. As I returned home from work, I saw him busy packing a suitcase in his room. I instantly assumed that he wanted to go on a trip like his mum and sister—this 'packing' antic was his way of making that point to me. I asked him casually, 'Where are you planning to go?'

Noel answered crisply, 'To the GK-1 Police Station; have to stay in the lock-up room for a few days, Baba.'

Flabbergasted, I asked, 'But why?'

Another crisp reply followed, 'Baba, I have done something wrong ... I broke a bowl in the kitchen today. Now drop me to the police station.'

This then is an illuminating example of his understanding that a wrong act must necessarily lead to punishment—there was never an intent of finding an escape to save himself. His world was indeed black and white—no shades of grey.

CHAPTER TEN

Let's Play Some Bad Tennis

One day, I was sitting on the large green patch behind the tennis wall practice area (a comfortable 1,500-square-foot area), splendidly encased by tall trees that reached for the clouds. While I was absorbing the quiet infinity of the sky, inhaling the pristine stillness away from the busy, noisy and cluttered life of Delhi, my mind travelled back in time to the beginning of the arduous journey of teaching Noel the elements of the artful game of tennis.

'Noel! Left foot forward. Bend a little. Now, look at the ball. Do not take your eyes off it! Swing the racquet, hit it back! Keep the racquet straight, face it forward. No, no—*yes*, like that. Now, swing it hard, show me a power shot. Come on, go for it, move it, man, move it! Concentrate, you have to focus, focus! That's it, the forehand, yes, a strong shot. Now backhand! You've got it! Excellent, proud of you—no, don't look away. Ah! You've missed the ball!'

And then, exasperatedly, 'You're not paying attention. Stop dreaming, Noel!'

Noel's equation with the sphere of sports was so very different compared to mine—a thought that nagged me all the time. He did not have the freedom to choose any game. There were constraints when it came to choosing one for him. I was his self-appointed trainer and settled on focusing on non-team games for Noel; namely, tennis, cycling and roller skating (besides his consistent pursuit of swimming). Squash and carom got added along the way.

I had been training him for fifteen years. Within the spectrum of various tennis shots that the boy had accomplished with amazing perseverance, the backhand returns deserve special mention. However, could Noel play the game as most boys do after so many years of coaching? The answer was a big no. The first thing I had to teach myself was to reconsider the notion of time periods that a child like Noel would take to learn and practice. So, fifteen years in the time scale would not be the same as it would be for a neurotypical person.

Comparisons would have been grossly misplaced, I know. However, in the initial years, I was instantly caught in the harrowing turbulence of comparing Noel with other boys and girls his age that came to play. My persistent worry was that it was an enormous loss of time to learn to play. Why was he unable to progress like every other kid? This thought ate away at me anytime I stepped into the play area.

There was such a difference in his disposition, motivation to learn and in the understanding of instructions as compared to others. It took me nearly five years to completely get rid of the urge to compare and the unbearable pain it caused me.

I always say reconciliation is a self-taught skill and that a dialogue with the self, furiously constructive, is the essence of bringing about change from within. Following a whole-hearted and gracious acceptance of Noel the way he was, the path forward became truly unstoppable. It released, perhaps, some new kind of chemicals in my physiology and a freshly positive energy appeared to have replaced that dreadful overflowing frustration.

I was able to reach a state of bliss when I was with Noel on the tennis courts. The duty-bound, committed, yet inwardly frustrated dad became a helplessly dependent one, turning to Noel for an injection of calm and elevation of the spirit. It was an intangible change ostensibly, but a sea change within. My son became the provider of comfort and relaxation at the end of a miserable day. When I was in a logjam with office politics or in financial upheaval, the person for me to run to was my boy, Noel. Surprisingly, the impact that emanated from the tennis wall practice began to radiate in every sphere of my life. Such was the power of acceptance.

The transition then to the next level of what I call supreme joy was easy and took an unbelievably short time. I must mention that I had had this vision that I would make Noel a good tennis player when we had started out. Nonetheless, if you re-imagine the yardstick to measure success, then Noel truly attained it. Gradually, he had overcome his distractibility, his penchant for non-stop self-talk, or his desire to spontaneously break into songs. Admittedly, some elements of that vision could not be realised—he still required me to escort him to his tennis practice. He could never be in practice all by himself.

This was around the same time that I had resolved that I would be able to coach him to break free of those heavy chains holding him back—his constantly wavering concentration and abrupt bursts of disinterest, that persistent wobble in his legs as he ran, his poor hand-eye coordination, his inconsistent strength, his speed of visual processing and so on. I had to learn about his physical and motor difficulties precisely by observing him, noting every detail and then formulating methods to leverage his relatively strong points amidst the plethora of deficits.

His difficulty also lay in comprehending the rules of the game—the scores, the concept of winning and losing, the boundary lines, the singles and doubles side-lines—even though the rules were laid out in a visually clear and structure-friendly way, for the boy, the meanings remained complex. So, here was a new lesson: everything that is structure-oriented may not always work because symbolic meanings were not always relatable.

The mountainous barrier that had to do with Noel's motivation also had to be overcome. A lack of interest in wanting to learn and the usual joy of figuring out a new trick or skill appeared to be almost absent. Then, how did I start?

I remember how we started. The first thing I had to teach a ten-year-old Noel was to mark out a fixed place in the wall practice area that he would serve from and come back to after fetching the ball.

I called it the 'position' and marked it with chalk. 'Noel, take position!' was my instruction, always given in a direct and business-like tone. I would also place a dry leaf on it. Why a dry leaf? Well, because when he had been a little boy walking in the nearby park, he would go around collecting the fallen leaves scattered around trees. It was an object of familiarity, and thus, likeable.

Later, I had the idea of adding an audio-signalling to the marked position. I placed a used Cola can lid so that when Noel put his right foot to take the playing stance, it would produce a mild screeching sound.

Next, I taught him how to grip the racquet handle. Noel could not clasp anything with his hands, nor could he calibrate his grip while he moved about the racquet. He started, but with a steadfast yet gentle grip. Teaching Noel to tighten the grip itself was clearly going to be a major first lesson. I realised that until you get down to specific movements and manual applications, the nature and extent of the gross and fine motor dysfunctions would never surface. His incapability of holding a pencil with his fingers firmly was known early enough at school and experimentation with a gripper to support his writing had already started. However, the hand-gripping issue surfaced only when we got started with tennis practice. So, 'Grip tight, Noel, try, try, keep trying ... let's see a firm grip ... grip tight!' became the next mantra that he had to grasp, and he did so quickly.

I would call out and hold his hand and walk him through the action of serving from his side, not over his head (not the classical tennis service) and then rally by hitting the ball back to the wall. Then I would ask him to show me the steps, one by one, without the ball. He would comply. I stuck to a sequenced approach.

Things moved forward. I would stand behind him a few metres away, performing the role of a ball boy as he started to serve or run to hit the ball that I had tossed from behind him, sometimes bouncing it off the wall.

Noel could not hit the ball off the wall. The ball rolled past him with every underhand serve and I had to dash in to field it. My childhood cricketing days came streaming back into my head while teaching Noel tennis. I retraced the actions and reflexive moves for good ground fielding and catching, just like I had done as a kid in the school's cricket grounds. It was such a joy to get a clean pick of the ball coming in chest or knee high. I developed this proclivity to find something for personal amusement as well while I ran around hollering in the practice zone like a man possessed.

Needless to add, I had to plan the timings so that Noel would be the only one playing in the practice area, although, in later years, he became accepting of others also practising alongside him.

There were times when Noel would just walk away and would not respond to anything I said. He was adamant and unwilling to go back to 'the position' to serve. A sudden disappearance of motivation. It was very difficult to trace it always to a trigger. Then, the only strategy I would resort to was a compromise. Regardless of what ABA (Applied Behaviour Analysis) experts say about its appropriateness, I used inducements to motivate Noel. A sandwich, a soda or a samosa would do the trick. But it was not frequent and only reserved for a bad day.

Sometimes he would break into song in the tennis practice area and in the later years, as he gradually became adept in the singing department, the frequency of song breaks increased. While he was belting out his favourite songs, he would simply become oblivious to all my commands. No targets, no competition, no frustration, only happiness in tennis, and yes, singing when you wanted to sing because you are happy—that was Noel's mantra.

Another unexpected obstacle was that Noel was generally scared of birds and always fearful that the low-flying birds would swoop down at any moment and hurt him. Quite often, the appearance of a flock of birds brought proceedings to a standstill. He would be petrified. There were days when nothing could be done because of birds hovering ceaselessly in the practice area. Over the next five years, Noel got over his fear of birds to a large extent. It took my constant reassurance (you had to keep going on like a broken record) that birds were harmless and only being playful.

Then there was a time after a year when I began searching for a coach who could take the practice forward with greater frequency, perhaps with a better methodology. There were a couple of coaches I tried for some sessions, but they had no clue about autism and wanted to see rapid progress like they saw in neurotypical children whom they regularly coached at various clubs.

The most important recognition in coaching a child with autism is that the needle of progress moves at an astonishingly slow speed. There may be many months of no forward movement. The reinforcements by way of repeated recall have to be issued for every basic step even after you have graduated to teaching a somewhat complicated level of tennis skills. In short, you would have to make sure that you start from the very beginning of every session. This is standard practice under any school teaching methodology but then for special education this has a bigger significance in learning; it provides emotional comfort for the child as they feel encouraged and motivated by the familiarity.

There were days when I would book a court to give Noel a taste of playing on a tennis court and hitting the ball over the actual net instead of hitting above the simulated net markings on the wall.

The bewildering thing about autism is that you never know what will suddenly crop up and spoil the party. One such scenario occurred when Noel, then twelve, cheerily trotted into the tennis court and started to serve as I stood on the opposite side to return the ball and call out the commands. He began hitting decent shots over the net; the shots were low in power but well-controlled. Things chugged along. We were enjoying the practice session in the bright, sun-drenched court. Suddenly, things went for a toss. The 40-foot-high wire mesh boundary wall that served as a separator between courts became the cynosure of Noel's eyes. There were these mesh separators between the tennis courts in the sports complex as they were laid out one after the other in a row. When you missed connecting the racquet with the ball, the ball would race to the wire mesh partition, making a loud jangling sound. Noel was excited to hear that sound. He always had an inexplicable attraction to funny or odd sounds with unusual patterns. Instead of hitting an oncoming ball back, the boy would let it pass so that he could hear the jangling sound when it struck the mesh. It filled him with so much delight! My commands were completely ignored in those moments.

Then Noel, instead of serving the ball to the opposite side of the tennis court, would turn around and start serving with all his might onto the wire mesh partition for the jangling sound. Nothing in the world could bring him back to playing across the net! What he relished was the long finish of the jangling; the way the wire mesh vibrated after the ball struck it.

Passers-by thought Noel was being an undisciplined brat. We could feel their stares of disapproval and annoyance. They seemed to wonder what kind of father I was; why was I not yelling at him and putting the whole thing to a halt? My first reaction, honestly, was to ask him to immediately stop, but I was sure that it would only spur him on, since to him, even anger or displeasure from me was a form of attention sometimes. He loved to push my buttons. And further, he believed he was not causing anyone harm. For him, it was something that was a lot of fun! And so, I would also join in and ignore the disapproval of strangers. Imagining the wire partition as the practice wall, I would serve the ball and both of us would laugh out loud with the jangle. Noel exclaimed, 'Baba, see this is fun!' while I pretended that I enjoyed that jangling sound as much as him.

After twenty minutes of such shenanigans, I would say, 'Noel, we will do this five more times and then move into the court.' This was my way of trying to give him a specific structure as a pathway to exit from distractions and get back to proper practice. This strategy worked and I began to apply it in many more situations. No showing of annoyance, no showing disapproval, no rebukes; letting him indulge but offering him a structure with a short time frame for him to exit the distraction.

Over the years of persistent rigour, Noel overcame all his deficiencies and started playing tennis on the courts like any twenty-year-old, albeit in an odd style. His shots and movements were not in the standard mould; he did not have the classic forehand, backhand or volley shots or the usual approach to moving around the court. Instead, he had a certain quirky approach in his swings and in-court striding. And I loved to watch that!

I used to often reflect on how the notion of quick success is such a ubiquitous demon. It needs serious self-examination and thought. The measure of grading success has to be recalibrated.

I also really had to teach myself the virtue of patience. Every time I got testy, I made it a point to say to myself that this was not okay, that I was being stupid. You cannot make a difference if you lose your cool. You have to coach yourself to be even-tempered through self-dialogue and set goals for your own behaviour vis-à-vis the child.

It was a realisation for me that coaching disabled or neurodiverse children or adults in sports always opens several doors for a whole host of learning opportunities in different areas for the child—social skills, daily living, numerical skills and language skills. This raises the quotient of 'enduring learning' that is much talked about by educators. So, tennis practice meant a lot of things for Noel. To evaluate his tennis practice by only examining his tennis capabilities and improvements would be a kind of short-sightedness. The markers of the evaluation would need to be different.

As time rolled by, I started finding the tennis wall practice area in the Siri Fort Sports Complex to be a great de-stressing zone of my own. It was tucked away in one corner of the 200-acre compound, far away from the weekend crowds. I would take my turn to practice my own shots once in a while, as Noel took a break to amble about or sit in the grass area and sing his favourite songs.

There were times when he would suddenly break into a classic Bollywood number just when he appeared to be ready for a serve, traversing mentally to another realm entirely. He would tune out my commands and, with his racquet firmly in his right hand and the ball in his left, standing still like a statue, he would sing aloud the fabulous melodies of Mohammad Rafi, Mukesh, Kishore Kumar and Lata Mangeshkar (*Piya Bina Basiya Baaje Na* from the Amitabh Bachchan and Jaya Bhaduri movie, *Abhimaan,* was always at the top of his singing list in tennis sessions). During those unstoppable singing reveries that went on for twenty or more minutes, I would watch him, amused and exasperated, hoping that he would quickly return to the game from his unstoppable, happy singing.

Noel's short-distance running eventually improved in the tennis practice area and that enabled better muscle coordination. His eye-hand coordination also improved and his racquet grip practice allowed for exercising calibration and manipulation of grip, improving motor coordination tremendously. To build on the latter improvements, Pia had the idea of introducing Noel to squash at the same sports complex. She became a regular with Noel on the squash courts. It was, broadly, an extension of the racquet movements of tennis, which she patiently supervised. No coach was really accessible to Noel during such developmental years, a harsh reality that we had accepted.

The other activity that Noel was inducted into was cycling. The steady improvement in racquet grip also helped to improve his grip on the cycle handles. A question that persisted was how do we teach him to slow down? The command, 'Now apply brakes!' did not always work well.

When I tried to teach him to brake while going down the slope, it proved to be a very difficult challenge. The gentle, gradual increase of the grip on the brakes as you go downhill was a hard lesson to impart. Initially, he could not comprehend the action and why that would slow down the cycle. I had to show him the braking rubber slabs and repeatedly explain the mechanical action. The jigsaw pieces came together for him. We achieved a small breakthrough! This, in my book, is an example of a micro-achievement that must be celebrated.

At the time we had started, he would refuse to cycle down slopy sections. He would always find a detour and escape the slopes. But once he understood the braking mechanics, there was no going back.

I would call it an unplanned therapeutic intervention that turned out to be so good for Noel's proprioception system. In other words, his neurological system's ability to make sense of multiple sensations and stimuli came together and sensory integration transpired. It made him ready to take on sharper slopes! So, one thing had led to another. The tennis racquet grip paved the way for better cycling and greater confidence.

I realised that even if the learning of tennis was not going in the right direction as per the conventional yardstick, there was a great deal of contentment to be derived from the fact that this was perhaps an excellent occupational therapy session, albeit done in an unconventional way.

So, there were other benefits that had accrued over those fifteen years. Yes, Noel did not become a tennis player at the same level as his peers who had started learning around the same time, but our father-son bond became stronger, as did the mother-son bond, thanks to the squash initiative.

When I used to be away on business travel, Noel would always end the video call with: 'Baba, when you are back, let's go for tennis. I want to play some bad tennis!' For Noel, bad tennis was more fun than good tennis! After all, and I'm sure many would agree, why do we always have to be good at things?

––––––

Once, during our routine cycling session, I was firing instructions to push Noel to the next level:

    'Now go through the space between the two cars parked there!'

    'Keep focused, look straight ahead.'

    'U-turn, please.'

'U-turn, again.'

'Sharp right.'

'Now a left and another U-turn.'

'Go fast! Fast!'

'Focus, focus Noel!'

I was at full throttle. Noel halted his cycle and looked at me with earnestness and in a low tone, devoid of any emotion of cockiness, bitterness or petulance, said, 'Dad, can we go home and do math on the calculator instead?'

In one swift blow, he had made it clear that I had taken the joy out of cycling and made it more arduous than mathematics.

———

In Noel's Sunday timetable, cycling was slotted as a must-do. One day, he flatly refused to go for it.

'Just what is the point in cycling?'

In my bid to motivate him, I enthusiastically explained how he would be able to travel to different places within Delhi all by himself. I named the malls he liked, the streets, favourite cafes ... when he interjected and asked, 'Can I cycle from Delhi to Kolkata and see Howrah bridge?'

I was honest and said no. At my refusal, what followed was a priceless facial expression that reiterated his original conviction: what's the point of putting in so much effort in mastering cycling?

———

Here's a short poem written by Noel's sister, then in the sixth grade. It's a piece that got published in the monthly magazine of her school.

A Precious Smile by Ahvana Paul

My special brother, Noel,
Hit hard the tennis ball
An uppish forehand aimed at the wall
But sadly, the ball curved over the wall
Oh noooo! shouted he
Rushing to the other side

His ball was to be seen nowhere
My anxious brother looked all around
And spotted his ball inside a greenhouse
The gate had a big lock
And nobody to be seen to talk
And then a yawning old guard was spotted
Seated so far away
Noel ran to him
Maybe he has the gate key?
Nahin hai ji!

And then surprise surprise,
A change of heart!
The sleepy guard's face lit up
A moment of good intention
He swung into action
To end Noel's tension

Climbing over that giant gate,
Swift, he was
Yippee! The ball was retrieved
Noel exclaimed
'Thank you, thank you, Guard ji!'
And none could stop Noel

Giving that bear hug to
The dear old guard

'Jab muskurahat itna kamal ka, Noel bhai,
tumhare liye toh hum hain hazir, always'
(When the smile is so beautiful, brother Noel,
for you, I shall always be there)
Said the guard, so warmly,
I think and wonder even today
Why is it that Noel's smile
Could be so precious?

CHAPTER ELEVEN

Breaking Hari Sir

We make promises all the time to meet old friends, colleagues or dear ones for a meal or a catch-up session over coffee. The plans are often meticulously made with the time, the right ambience and a convenient venue decided in advance. Despite such planning, there are people who can never keep their promises to meet. There is always the habitual last-minute ditcher. But as we go along with life, we learn to handle the disappointments and quickly get over them. Our expectations for that person change but we also learn to condone the ditcher with grace even when we know the excuses are lame. However, everything changes when you are dealing with a person like Noel. For him, a promise made constituted a future 'structure' cast in stone to be delivered without fail.

In the middle of a cold winter night, I suddenly heard Noel's panicky scream. 'Baba! Baba! I have broken Hari Sir! Yes! Yes! I have broken him!'

I woke up with a start and switched on the bedside lamp. Noel, then nineteen, was standing by the side of my bed, trembling. His face was white with fear. I sat up, my eyes barely open. That early parenting lesson of being gentle and making sure your tone is adequately soft at all times when the child's tone gets excited and high-pitched reverberated through my head.

So gently, placing my hand on his shoulder, I asked him, 'Noel, what are you talking about?' I saw him crouch in fear and his guilt-filled eyes shone through even in partial darkness. A familiar alarm rang in my head. Something must have gone terribly wrong. He shook his head and repeated, 'Baba, I have really broken Hari Sir.' A longish pause followed this. And then: 'Forever!'

Holding my hand, he walked me to the drawing room, switched on the light and pointed towards the brilliantly coloured, foot-and-a-half-tall statuette of a harlequin on our shiny white table top. As I looked closer, I realised that the statue of the clown stood headless and then I spotted the separated head on the table surface. It had been neatly twisted out of the body with the hat on the head and the black mask all intact. It was an unusual act of aggression by the boy and it was a disturbing sight.

My first reaction was to give him the shouting of a lifetime. Then, looking at him, I realised that the boy was immersed in guilt. My temptation to tear into him had to be controlled. I calmed myself with considerable effort.

'Why are you talking about Hari Sir?'

'I broke Hari Sir!'

Bewildered, I held up the harlequin in my hand, 'This?'

'Yes, that is Hari Sir!'

Hari Sir had been one of Noel's favourite teachers from his school but had suddenly left for a new job at a school in Abu Dhabi. That had been six years ago. When he'd quit his job in the special section of the school, Noel had suffered a lot. He had always been deeply attached to his teachers, all of them, and Hari Sir had been a favourite. So, when he left Noel in the proverbial lurch, the boy experienced a lot of pain and anguish.

Unfortunately, the impact of the sudden exit of any person close to Noel had never been considered a situation of importance and something that he should have been prepared for in advance, either by Noel's school or by us. There hadn't been any strategy prepared for such contingencies. Noel's vulnerable mind struggled to deal with unexpected exits of people close to him in his daily life and we did not grasp that or the extent of the heartbreak he'd undergo due to a lack of proper closure; we did not consider then the question of how he will cope in the coming days.

So, over the next six years, almost every week without fail, Noel would bring up Hari Sir in obsessive monologues. He used to narrate the details of many little interactions that he had had with him at school. He would enumerate the long list of things he would want to do that Hari Sir would say 'no' to. There was also the oft-repeated tale about the times Noel would raid Hari Sir's lunchbox. He recounted all this in a storytelling style that ended with a chuckle and an exclamation in Bengali, '*Ki moja holo*, Baba (What fun that was, dad)!'

I, on the other hand, would get quite fed up with the Hari Sir stories but forced myself to turn my irritability into a constructive strategy aimed to open his mind to something new.

'Let's see where Hari Sir lives now. See, these are pictures of Abu Dhabi,' I would say. I was only trying to break through the obsessive merry-go-round thought patterns that refused to stop or change direction. This also allowed me to explore the internet with Noel, helping me display and demonstrate Google as an image search engine, and he quickly picked up on the logos and the various visual icons. He was quite impressed by the stunning seaside images and the splendid tall buildings of Abu Dhabi and once asked, 'Baba, can I make a trip to Abu Dhabi?'

'Sure, Noel, you can go. I will buy you tickets and Hari Sir can come to the Abu Dhabi airport and pick you up. You can stay with him and you can go along with him to his special school. He might take you to a good place for South Indian food,' I responded.

'No Baba, I can't go alone. I don't know the direction.'

Engaging him momentarily in other tracks of thought was possible and his anxiety would subside. He would engage in self-talk, 'Baba will also go with me. Baba plus Noel to Abu Dhabi! Okay? Okay.'

So, it was possible to penetrate that circuitous thought pattern that had taken firm root and use the break to bring in other appropriate emotional elements.

To continue with the story that led to the assault of the harlequin statue in the living room—one day, after six years, Hari Sir suddenly arrived in Delhi. Noel and I were excited to talk to him on the phone. Noel was very sentimental on the phone, as was expected. 'Hari Sir, can you come to my house and watch TV? We will watch Al Jazeera. I will also bake a brownie for you! Or we could meet at Starbucks?' (Al Jazeera was my favourite channel so he thought it was a cool channel to watch and one that must interest everybody).

A few days later, Noel had just accompanied me to the Honda body repair shop in Okhla—he was mesmerised by the variety of repair work and impressed by the mechanics. Their skills in fixing badly damaged cars, in his eyes, made them demigods. Repairing cars and making them look like new after accidents was an act of genius!

He was also quite taken in by the special air-conditioned lift used for the cars to be moved across floors and the well-appointed customer lounge where we were served coffee.

'Baba, this place is good. Can we meet Hari Sir here, in this lounge ... and not Starbucks?'

I was thrilled at how he was stringing sentences together and communicating meaningfully. It was also true that Noel was not lacking in motivation if you dug beneath the outer surface. There had to be a steady nudge from us to help him apply himself in constantly adding to expressive communications. He needed that stimulant. Even if he did not comply after persuading him a hundred times, resignation was never an option.

In anticipation of the meeting with Hari Sir, Noel used to break into a loud monologue for hours. There was irony surrounding this because I knew that much would not happen in terms of communication exchange when the anxiously awaited face-to-face meeting did take place. There would be none of the animated chatter and sharing of experiences that we are so used to, taking turns in conversation, loud laughter, witty remarks and recounting of anecdotes; the usual fare in our social catch-ups. But nor would there be any awkward silences. Maybe Noel would break into a song by ABBA or Celine Dion. That was how things were in Noel's world of love.

The day arrived. Noel and I were all set for the grand rendezvous. But then, Hari Sir called up and cancelled an hour before the appointed time. Noel erupted. I had a solid challenge of pacifying the boy as he suddenly, for the first time, resorted to self-harming behaviour.

A new date was fixed with Hari Sir to come over to our place. Yet again, he cancelled on the appointed day, saying that he had had gotten injured after having fallen on the road. This time, when I shared this with Noel, his first reaction was one of deep concern for Hari Sir. There was no implosion. Worried, he told me he wanted to talk to Hari Sir immediately. He made me dial him and Noel enquired about his injury and how his beloved teacher was coping. It was a soulful and warm exchange.

For Noel, these meet-up structures were sacrosanct. The most efficient way to alleviate his distress was to draw stick figures and verbally explain the reasons for cancellation.

This was a technique I had devised by taking a leaf out of the TEACCH methodology to tackle such situations.

Every day, without fail, Noel enquired about Hari Sir. From his non-stop monologue, I could fathom that he was conjuring up images of Hari Sir in a hospital, getting injections, with doctors attending to his injury and being plastered. He would suddenly exclaim in the middle of a tennis practice session, 'Hari Sir has gone for a change of plaster today!'

Many days rolled by. There was no call from Hari Sir, nor did he answer his phone. Noel kept badgering me to try and I left many messages but there was never any reply. The boy was heartbroken and there were no signs of his distress receding with the passage of days. We never heard from the teacher again.

The surrogate assault on the harlequin figure was but a manifestation of being let down by Hari Sir. His unexpressed hurt and anguish needed an outlet. As the adage goes, experience is the best teacher. Noel had learnt a little more about the harshness and indifference of our real world through this episode.

———

The film, Rain Man, *won eight Oscars in 1989. Dustin Hoffman won Best Actor for his stellar performance as the protagonist, Raymond, an autistic savant. The character is based on the real-life Rain Man, Kim Peek, a gifted autistic person who lived with his father till he passed away some years ago at the age of fifty-six. Hoffman, after winning the Oscar, had gone to meet Kim, handed the trophy to him and asked his father to 'share him with the world' so that awareness could be built around autistic savants.*

One amusing scene from the film is when someone asks the protagonist, 'What does your date look like, Raymond?' Raymond answers, 'She looks like a holiday.'

To my astonishment, Noel once used a similar descriptor, 'She's like Sunday!' for a dear befriender, Tanya, when I asked him about her after they'd spent time sitting on the park bench, listening to their favourite music and chatting. A pithy descriptive.

———

One person whom Noel, seventeen, grew very fond of, perhaps had a crush on, was Evonne, twenty-one, from Cologne, Germany. She stayed with us as a paying guest for four months. She was in Delhi for an internship as a part of her course to become a schoolteacher.

Noel was always very conscious of her presence and always tried to be calm and well-mannered. One day in the living room, I saw Noel singing songs for her. After she returned to Cologne, Noel would talk about her and often imagine that Evonne would come to Delhi someday to visit him, and how he would go to the airport to receive her. Or if her flight was delayed, Noel would wonder then what he would do. He'd mutter about how he would sit in the waiting lounge and have coffee and 'read a magazine or something'. Perhaps he'd show her the Qutub Minar and the Lodhi Gardens. But Evonne's second visit to Delhi never happened. However, Evonne would send a gift hamper for Noel every Christmas and remained forever his most admired young lady.

———

There are some actresses that have a kind of timeless beauty and charisma whom many individuals of successive generations invariably have a crush on.

For me, it was Audrey Hepburn. I fell head over heels after watching that magnificent movie Roman Holiday. Undoubtedly, this is a common experience many go through. Even now, I have a framed picture of her with a long cigarette holder in my study from Breakfast at Tiffany's.

Once, I discovered young Noel had removed that picture from the wall in the study and placed the frame near his bed. I asked him, puzzled, 'Why is Audrey here?'

The boy replied wryly, 'She is giving me company. I like Audrey Hep-Burn.'

CHAPTER TWELVE

Thank You for the Music

In 2017, there used to be a television advertisement featuring Bollywood actor Ranbir Kapoor for Renault's new SUV. The ad showcased the car rather well and did persuade me to go into the nearest showroom for a test drive. Noel used to be my natural ally for such showroom visits.

Accompanied by a courteous sales attendant, I embarked on the test drive, Noel in tow. In a few minutes, as I drove out onto the main road, Noel shot a question to the sales attendant, 'Is there no CD player?' He was attempting to turn up the volume, bending over from the back seat to reach the dashboard.

The sales attendant replied jovially, 'This is a new-generation car, sir, only pen drive or mobile input! Listen to the sound, it's fantastic!'

Noel did not appear happy with the explanation.

When we got back to the showroom for the usual sale discussions, the salesmen were pampering Noel, asking him which colour option would he prefer and generally behaving as if the sale was 99 per cent in their pocket and that the only thing left was Noel's nod. With all the attention showered on him, Noel was feeling gleefully self-important. He was enjoying being addressed as 'sir' and being served coffee and biscuits with much pomp and cordiality. I had to haul him out of the showroom.

We started our drive home and Noel popped the question: 'Why did you not buy the car?'

Wryly, I asked him what he thought was the reason. I always pushed him to string together the reasons in his mind and express himself with whatever vocabulary he had. In my head, I was readying my explanation of how the price was unjustified and how the key features fell short of other new SUVs.

Noel answered in a grim tone, 'Because ... because no CD player!'

For him, if one cannot insert physical music CDs into a stereo player, then there is not much sense in having a car, however swanky it may appear. The virtual space of ownership did not fit into his needs of the real. He needed to physically possess his favourite music titles only as CDs, feel them in his hands, title by title. Noel could listen to a single song a hundred times in a loop or have the same CD run again and again in the car music system.

Noel was drawn to music at a very early age. Even though he had not previously heard the words actually in usage per se, as he listened to songs, he would articulate the new words from the lyrics just as he heard them, word by word, in the exact tune. He never failed to get the tune right, not even the first time that he sang a song! It was astonishing and appeared to be a natural gift. Also, he was blessed with a good voice with considerable variation in pitch and the right baritone for melodic compositions.

When Noel was six, he started with Disney's *Children's Favourites* and they remained his favourites even when he turned twenty-six! They were his comfort music in times of loneliness or stress. He sang them all, from volumes 1-4, in the exact sequence as they appeared in the albums right through his childhood and adult years. Music worked like a balm beyond compare. It went beyond being a private, self-directed pacifier, opening a new door for social exchanges.

His first question would be 'Do you have songs on your mobile phone?' and if he had heard a song on that person's mobile phone on an earlier occasion, then the next questions would follow: 'Can I listen to *Super Trouper* by ABBA on your phone, please? After that, I want to listen to *Thank You for the Music*, please. What is your favourite song, friend? Can you sing it?' and when the same question was posed to him, Noel would gladly oblige. Yes, he could instantaneously sing a song for you.

Then YouTube arrived, followed by the iPad which lit up his life like no other object. Music videos became a new and fascinating indulgence for Noel. He picked up and remembered every visual detail in the music videos. Also, he could watch a single video many times over. It was obviously a stimulatory experience and his innate trait of desiring repetitiveness was thoroughly indulged. His engagement with this sea of audio-visual enthrallment appeared to simply envelop him and he could be at it for five or six hours at a stretch. Also, my hunch was that he liked that a particular song is sung the same way every time it plays and the visuals sync with the track which fed unfailingly into the autistic appetite for sameness. The unchanging melody structure, the same musical instruments, the same pauses and effects, the same images in sequence brought him a certain calm and became the sure-shot resource to turn to whenever he used to get stressed and a tantrum was brewing or, on a more serious note, approaching a meltdown. No mood stabiliser medicines were required if music was at hand.

This inspired us to use songs to coach him in language skills, to describe situations he experienced and teach him the concept of one experience resembling another. I was cautiously optimistic that such techniques, along with adroit questioning, would lead to more articulate and expressive communications. Such unconventional methods of teaching became a matter of routine at home.

Noel's love for music soon segued into an obsession with the game of *antakshari* (with Bollywood songs) when a friend, who also became his free-hand exercise instructor, introduced him to it. Once he had understood the ask, he became rather proficient and would traverse between Hindi and Bengali songs, playing *antakshiri* for hours.

Then a related development happened: when he heard a conversation going on near him that he was not part of, he would pluck a word from that conversation and sing a song starting with the exact word chosen. It was precise; the song just appeared on Noel's lips, automatically.

Singing as an expressive communication skill eventually reached a higher level: to express his opinion via a song or a segment of the song, he would invariably pick an apt one and sing aloud as a form of commentary on the situation at hand! On one instance, when our car braked and screeched to a halt to avoid a collision with an oncoming autorickshaw from the opposite side, Noel, sitting by my side, broke into an old classic from the '70s, in full volume, '*E! Bhai zara dekh key chalo, aagey bhi nahin, peechey bhi, dayine bhi nahin, baayen bhi … upar hi nahin, neecheybhi … e! Bhai zara dekh key chalo* (Hey! Bro, just watch a bit and move, not just in front, the rear side too, not just the right side, the left side also, not just what's above you but also what's beneath you).' It was so whimsical to see him sing on cue!

There was a leap in his singing skills every year, particularly through his late teens and his memory for tunes and song lyrics. As he matured in the music department, many more amusing tales filled my treasure house of memories.

Noel had seated himself in the movie hall to watch his much-admired singer's biopic, *Rocketman*. After about an hour of watching, humming and singing along, just when I began to think what a relief it was to see him in sync with everything and in a state of rare contentment, Noel stood up all of a sudden and announced, 'I am finished.'

'The movie has not finished. Just sit down!' said Ahvana sternly.

'I am finished!'

Forcefully, he was made to sit. Then the answer came like a shaft of light in that darkness!

Noel, in tears, asked, 'When will "Baby has got blue eyes, blue, blue day ... and she is alone again ... and I am home again" happen?'

Sir Elton John, the Rocketman, had disappointed him on that occasion!

Autism researcher, Pamela Heaton, Professor of Psychology, Goldsmiths University of London has shown that not just the savants, but even non-savant children with autism possess a great deal of musical potential that can be developed and channelised productively. Other researchers have observed that the affective quality of musical experiences is not muted in any way for the keen listener on the autism spectrum. In contrast to their performance within social and interpersonal domains, children with autistic disorders showed no deficits in processing the effect of musical stimuli.* It plays out differently for different people, but the overarching learning is that music must be a part of a child's development plan. It can be imaginatively integrated into learning systems at home, at school, or at a work or training centre. It can be a steady therapeutic aid, as well as a crucial academic teaching aid; a vehicle for social interactions and social skill development. The magnitude of

---

*'Can children with autistic spectrum disorders perceive affect in music? An experimental investigation' *Psychological Medicine, 1999, 29, 1405-1410, Cambridge University Press.*

its value in enhancing the child's inner sense of self-worth and self-confidence and, in the long run, providing eternal companionship, according to me, is beyond measure.

On the eve of a New Year celebration, I found Noel absorbed in songs by Kishore Kumar from a video of a concert uploaded on YouTube that ran for several hours. Noel sang along to every song that Kishore da chose to sing in the recorded show.

He sang along to the movie *Kora Kagaz's* title song, a song drenched in existentialist angst: '*Mera jivan kora kagaz ... kora hi rahe gaya ... udtey panchi ka thikana ... jaana hai mujhe kahan ... jo likha tha ansoon ... o ... ke sang bahey gaya* (My life is akin to a blank paper. It has remained blank ... the flying birds have no address ... where is my destination? Whatever had been written, has been washed away in my tears).'

Noel said, with a pained expression, 'Stop! No *ansoon*! Never *ansoon* (No tears, never tears)!' The word '*ansoon*' in the song was the trigger; he had learnt that shedding tears wasn't an acceptable act.

The Children's Favourite series from Disney, Noel's comfort music, induced the whole family to appreciate the collection much more than when we had heard these songs in our growing-up years. I rediscovered the brilliant lyrics, the tunes, the metaphors used. Of all the songs, I remember very well, the song that Noel had the richest imagery of that was linked with the memory of his four grandparents was *My Grandfather's Clock.*

While listening to this American classic (written by the famous ballad writer of his day, Henry Clay Work, in 1876) Noel would have this urge to talk about his Utpal Dadu, Dadabhai, Didaan and Thamma. It really brought alive the world of his grandparents right before his eyes. He was entranced whenever the song started to play and towards the end, he would start talking about each of his grandparents and what he would serve them if they came over to a tea party that he would host for them. He would chatter away about his maternal grandmother and his antics. She was driven up the wall by him from the time he was a toddler, and through the next seven years, as he ceaselessly used his colouring crayons on the walls of her living room and dining area. She used to go berserk. When nothing could prevent him from being that avant-garde child artist of wall art, she finally surrendered, 'Alright, this house will belong to you in the future, so please do what you want to! I give up!' Concerning his paternal grandmother Noel would reminisce about how she would serve him custard pudding whenever he arrived at her place. All the grandparent stories would roll in one after another whenever the legendary song came on. The way one song could evoke such affection and recall, sparking his imagination, was quite amazing.

Noel was very fond of ABBA songs and, as luck would have it, the movie *Mamma Mia! Here We Go Again* (2018) had started showing in a nearby movie hall. Going to a movie with his mother, sister or me was a rare treat for Noel. He loved to do so. As I entered the movie hall with him, I told him he could sing along from his corner seat, karaoke style, and how exciting it would be when the ABBA songs came up in the movie. In minutes, I realised I had lit a fire under my seat.

'Baba, where is the mic? How will I sing along?' Noel was insistent, flustered and began to whine about why had I not remembered to bring the karaoke microphone if I wanted him to sing along. The movie had not even started. I stormed out of the hall to fetch something to eat so that the boy would be distracted. However, popcorn and cola were rendered useless. The focus had become the new structure of 'singing along, karaoke style, with a hand mic'. The backdrop to this odd situation is that he had become quite used to singing with a mic at home so how the hell was he to sing along with the movie songs without a mic!

Sitting next to Noel during a 'structure-gone-awry' moment was very unsettling. People were staring. I resorted to a reasonable explanation, 'Noel, in movies, actors do not sing into mics, so please calm down, you can sing like them with no mic.' This pacified Noel.

The movie started. The calm remained for just five minutes! Because just then, the lead star, Lily James, in the very first scene, snatched the hand mic from the graduation ceremony announcer on the stage and broke into the first song, *When I Kissed the Teacher*. I swallowed hard. It was another blooper on my part.

Noel instantly turned and stared daggers at me. It was the one time I wished I had not got him to the movies.

———

The word 'pyaar' (love) is generously sprinkled in most Bollywood songs; this is universally known. Once, I asked Noel what is the English word for 'pyaar'? Noel said, 'Happy!'

I guess his interpretation was that the answer is his emotional connection with the word, not the literal meaning. In his world, this was the approach to take.

————

When I joked that Noel should thank YouTube and the iPad as they are his constant leisure companions, he surprised me by spontaneously singing the ABBA song:

> *Thank you for the music*
> *I'm nothing special, in fact, I'm bit of a bore*
> *But I have a talent, a wonderful thing*
> *'Cause everyone listens when I start to sing*
> *All I want is to sing it out loud*
> *So I say, thank you for the music*
> *Without the songs I am singing*
> *What would life be?*

————

Noel, twenty-two, was to meet his former schoolteacher, Mallika, thirteen years after she'd moved overseas. I was accompanying Noel to the café where they were to meet. The first thing he said as he greeted her with joyful excitement was, 'The song that was playing in my Blue Corsa was Kal Ho Na Ho! And the dessert served was gajar ka halwa!' Noel was dredging up memories from her wedding, fourteen years ago, in lieu of a greeting. Mallika was naturally surprised.

Noel had carried a gift for Mallika and he was treated to a slice of cake at the café. After we exchanged goodbyes, Noel said quizzically, 'Baba, I did not get a return gift?'

A slice of cake marks a special occasion, like a birthday celebration, this was embedded in Noel's mind. By implication, this occasion had to be a birthday. The return gift, to Noel, was a mandatory detail of a birthday celebration. The monster called 'linear structure' had cast a shadow over the reunion with his teacher.

––––––

It was the Aam Aadmi Party's public celebration of their stunning victory in the Delhi Assembly elections, winning almost 90 per cent of seats. It was also a long journey for Noel and I—metro and then a cab ride. Yes! I had braved the arduous journey to the Ram Lila maidan to witness the celebrations that would give a new kind of exposure to the young man.

Noel settled into his seat, looked around and observed, 'This is not Aam Aadmi Party ... it's Aam Aadmi Concert.' To him, the atmosphere had the feel and look of a concert, so it couldn't have been a party. In his lexicon, there is only one meaning for the word 'party' and all along, poor Noel had been expecting to attend one.

However, he did not leave disappointed. Towards the end of his speech, the new Chief Minister of Delhi, Arvind Kejriwal, sang the Manna Dey classic: 'Insan ka ho insan se bhaichara, yehi paigam hamara....dharti par ho pyar ghar ghar ka ujiyara...yehi paigam hamara (My message is for brotherhood amongst people and love in every home).'

Noel instantly found the similarity of the tune with 'Yeh desh ki dharti, sona ugle ... (This land of my country spews gold)' and stood up spontaneously in the middle of a thousand audience members and joined in, singing at the highest decibel, the patriotic song from the age-old Bollywood film, Upkaar. It was a magical moment; people near his seat started clapping and cheering him on! I had a bemused smile stuck on my face all the time for the next few hours till we reached home.

———

Manish Sisodia, beloved leader, Aam Aadmi Party, tweeted, '... is liye Delhi ke log kahe rahein hai 5 saal Kejriwal! (... that's why the people of Delhi are saying five years for Kejriwal!)' on the eve of the Delhi 2015 Assembly Elections. My son, Noel, the unlikely soothsayer, trumps the AAP leader and shouts, 'Bees saal Kejriwal (Twenty years for Kejriwal)!' upon joining the public rally in South Delhi.

The real reason that Noel exclaimed twenty years, the reason he genuinely thinks he deserved more than five years was simply because Kejriwal was a good singer. That for him was the hallmark of a good man.

CHAPTER THIRTEEN

Yes, Boss!

What was to happen after school?

Noel would not be appearing for any school board examination and would have no academic certificate. Nor would he have any manual or computer skills of a high order. The daily living tutoring and routine functioning skills would be a good foundation for him but had nothing to do with specific skills or any preparation for a conventional qualification that he could acquire upon leaving school. The pursuit of formal academics at any kind of level was also not meant for him. With his exit from school looming over us, I became obsessed with the idea of figuring out a way of providing Noel early work-life exposure while he was still cruising through his last couple of years in school, so that his transition into a sheltered vocational learning space would be a bit easier. But to be ready for that would be no small task. He would have to learn to accept a drastically unfamiliar environment, new people, new social dynamics and so on. And he would also have to learn new manual skills to be able to work eventually in a commercial establishment or a similar sort of set-up.

My anxiety about preparing for the future was propelling me to test what was possible and what was not, but I wasn't sure where to start, which is always a concern for many parents of children on the autism spectrum. I wanted to first check the two areas of interest where he was likely to have a high degree of innate motivation: automobiles and food.

When you are the parent of a child with a disability, you are mentally occupied with various questions and a wide set of concerns. The ones that gnawed at me the most were:

- What does it mean to be in a workplace?
- What does it mean to be doing things in the presence of so many unknown people around you?
- What is it like to be at the centre of the hustle-bustle that characterises a commercial kitchen or a car service garage?
- Would the situation induce the child to feel responsible and help him inculcate the disciplinary rigours of a workplace?
- Would he be mindful of the social context and restrain his loud singing or loud self-talk?
- Would he be able to take instructions from his supervisors?
- Would he have the good fortune to get a job coach he is comfortable with?

- Would he be able to manage himself and stay focused for a stretch of time all by himself?
- What about the sudden eruptions of stim behaviours triggered by monotony?
- What about going to the washroom? If the toilet was not spotlessly clean, he would refuse to use it. I would have to ensure that one person on the staff would volunteer to usher him to a clean washroom, using our usual prompt. An unusual maze to navigate!

The question of abusive behaviour on the part of the staff members also clouded my mind, but I consciously placed that on the back burner. We were going to have to play by the ear.

Noel was sixteen. My anxiety levels were only rising. I was determined to start the initiation of his exposure to a workplace and it had to be done after school hours. My persistent search helped me find a relatively new bakery run by a kindly soul, Arun, in Gurgaon, in a good old-world shopping area (as opposed to a mall). Arun had quit his job at an upscale hotel to start his own business; he was in his mid-thirties, gentle-natured, warm, open-minded and enthused to help Noel get his exposure in a commercial workplace. I told Noel that Arun was going to be his 'boss'. Noel was very amused with the idea of having a boss. Till this point in life, he thought having a boss was an exclusive privilege that only I enjoyed! Often, I used to excuse myself from an engagement with him on the grounds that my boss had asked me to do something, i.e., 'I cannot play tennis today, Noel, my boss has asked me to finish some urgent work'. But now, Noel had to be initiated into understanding the dynamics of a boss-related structure well in advance.

I had explained to Arun that Noel needed a consistent and visually sequential plan for his three-hour traineeship at the bakery after school and that it should require simple, short prompts from him to carry out the tasks. Arun decided that he should start in the backroom to assist with finishing the decorative garnishing on customised cakes and help with arranging the loaves of bread before customers came in.

For practice at home, we also mirrored the tasks in a commercial kitchen around that time. A job coach began working with Noel in our house. A small kitchen as a learning area was added to the new apartment exclusively for Noel. He learnt simple skills such as cutting and chopping vegetables and fruits, applying cheese, making sandwiches and learning the steps of how to make a brownie using the electric oven. By doing so, the basic familiarisation and a work orientation of sorts were accomplished satisfactorily with this set-up at home.

Within a couple of months, Noel was ready to start. Though it meant a long drive of more than an hour from his school in Delhi to the bakery in Gurgaon, Noel was visibly excited with the idea of working in a bakery. However, there was one huge hurdle that was yet to be crossed. How would we get Noel to restrain himself from picking up and eating the pastries, the brownies, the muffins and other favourites from the shelves in the backroom while working?

There had already been much discussion about how, in the

workplace, he cannot pick up food for personal consumption, but for Noel, a mere sermon about social behaviour would not work. It had to be hinged on a clear, understandable and compelling reason that had a layer of relatable emotion. 'Noel, you cannot eat the cakes and pastries because they are only for customers' was the strategic prompt I had selected to restrain him.

I repeatedly instructed him, so you can see there was a small element of rote learning (through repeated instructions), plus a bit of logical reasoning that he could grasp and a fair bit of empathy creation for the customer. The structure spelt out was sacrosanct and Noel fell in line with amazing discipline and restraint. The notion of a customer and the role of sales attendants or managers was something he had understood since the early days of car showroom visits that seemed to be wired into his brain. The idea that one had to care for the customer was drilled in with success. The other aspect of our strategy was that Noel would be given a tiffin box and that he could eat his tiffin outside the bakery after he had finished his work.

And so his work life began! And Noel got into the groove rather well.

Simultaneously, I explored the automobile-related vocation as well and visited several car companies, met with their HR departments and talked to their service section managers to explore the possibilities for inducting Noel through the methods of sequencing or setting simple routine structures to perform basic tasks. I suggested car washing activity; the manual aspects of which he could be exposed to before gradually shifting to assist in running the automated part of the process. The car service garages attached to major showrooms refused on the grounds of safety (a justified roadblock) and while they had no awareness about autism, they patiently listened to me with empathy and understood the challenges of autism in a workplace.

It had been about three months when suddenly, Noel's happy run came to an abrupt end due to an unfortunate development in the bakery.

With Noel having learnt the basic skills and settling into the workplace with all the adult co-workers who comprised a small team of six, the job coach's role was over within a few weeks and he did not accompany him anymore. One day, as Noel finished work and was about to leave, the store supervisor, who had built a rapport with him, said, 'Noel, you did very good work today! Here's a muffin, you deserve it! Your reward! Take it.'

Noel was happy, but confused since his Baba had told him these were all meant for customers and that he could not eat them. Nonetheless, he accepted his reward after some hesitation. Unfortunately, the rule that all the products on display were for customers was broken as a result of this. The next day after he finished his work, he unabashedly went to the display shelf of muffins in the shop and picked out two pieces to eat. The supervisor got annoyed, telling him it was not okay to do so. The man did not realise that his actions on the previous day had led to this. No logical reasoning would help reverse it. There was no stopping him now. This episode reinforced yet again that structures are sacred and there was no messing with them.

The out-of-line behaviour by Noel could not be remedied.

The boy had to quit the bakery. Many lessons were learnt there. Noel suffered a brief trauma after the 'sacking' but he got to learn the concept of being sacked for non-compliance!

However, the incident filled me with humiliation and anger. Arun, the owner, had to endorse the supervisor's decision, even though he understood it was not Noel's fault. This represents many a situation where people are not willing to be flexible and adjust to disabled people at the workplace. Lack of empathy, tolerance and understanding of supposed misconduct will come up many a time for parents as they bring the individual into the harsh real world. It is a fairly common challenge that one has to be prepared to encounter across many life situations. You have to find the reserve of mental toughness to recover from such crushing blows. In retrospect, this 'fall' actually made him far more adaptive in the future at places of work. Noel's takeaway from that incident was clear to him and this proved to be a blessing in disguise.

As he crossed eighteen, Noel left school. On that rather emotional occasion, Pia and I requested some of his teachers to meet him occasionally as he would now become friendless. He had not been able to make any friends amongst his peers in all those years at school. But the silver lining was that his equations with his teachers were akin to strong friendships. Their intermittent companionship would certainly help in alleviating the effects of the shift from a secure school environment to an atmosphere that was altogether different.

Noel joined a vocational training centre in Delhi. He started to get trained in various skills under job instructors. I pursued getting an internship at a popular pizza restaurant chain. The breakthrough came about! Noel became an intern, the first adult with autism in Delhi at a pizza restaurant and was to start in the kitchen as an assistant.

Noel's induction to the pizza outlet was a well-organised process—we took the staff through a collective presentation as to what the condition of autism meant and how Noel was challenged in many aspects. Thus, the implications of what they should expect and how they should react to him and verbally communicate with him were explained lucidly and jointly by the head of the vocational centre and me. The staff members were keen to gain awareness so it all worked out exceedingly well.

After the session, I remember I blurted out a very unexpected question that had bobbed into my head: if Noel wanted to take a nap suddenly during work, will there be a place? With all his social and communication impairments and the bundle of sensory needs he had, we had to make him feel safe and non-threatened in this new environment. The manager understood the unusual request and thoughtfully arranged for a small bed in the well-lit store room without any fuss. I was pleased since he would need that during the first 4-5 weeks as a settling-in mechanism. The need for it would gradually disappear, I assured them.

Noel did surprisingly well in various kitchen-support tasks and the dexterity of his fingers improved tremendously. He also began singing at work and within a few days, the staff had got used to this and nobody ever asked him to stop singing. They seemed to like the fact that there was always a song on Noel's lips.

With the basics of an adaptation to a workplace now covered, I was keen to take his exposure and skillset to another level and arranged for him to simultaneously start working in the packaging department at a fashion garment manufacturing house twice a week. Noel's innate skill for visual orderliness and sequential tasks gave him a head start and finger dexterity was a consistent strength I had noticed (thanks to his tennis and kitchen skills), so working on the tags that go on each garment piece on the shop floor and other micro-tasks concerning packaging came easily to him. The most important victory that was achieved was his calm behaviour in a scenario where lots of workers were constantly moving about him, chattering at close quarters.

Noel started producing work with precision and consistency. Credit goes to his job coach, Shamim, who implemented the strategy of breaking each task into sub-tasks and then ensuring consistent concentration without issuing threats or reprimands, even giving him breaks to sing. Prompts such as 'Try again, try again' in a kind, considerate and unhurried tone worked fabulously with the young man.

Noel had a history of losing interest if he was put under performance pressure or for reasons of monotony and Shamim was cognisant of that, making serious efforts to ensure that Noel's enthusiasm for the job could be sustained. Noel's supervisors were also briefed to interact with him for brief timespans and then leave him alone to move forward with his work. He needed to have the space to apply himself and gain a sense of importance. This worked well—I'd also learnt as a coach to Noel that he responds best to minimal instructions; the fewer words used, the better!

In a matter of months, Noel suddenly found himself running an hour-to-hour packed work schedule through the week. I was so pleased with what he had achieved post-school in the workplace.

An interesting thing that Noel would reminisce about often was how he had been sacked at the bakery. He'd say, with amusement, '*Mera naukri chala jayega!* (I will lose my job!) Never, never would want that to occur again.' And thus, he would be at his best behaviour in workplaces, insisting quite seriously to anyone around, 'I always listen to my boss. I always say, "Yes boss!"'

What was heartening was that there grew a sense of palpable self-dignity; a sense of pride in being able to do his assigned tasks satisfactorily, bringing an additional dimension to his personality and attitude.

Often, in the parents' circle, others would wonder, 'Why is this man so happy about his son working on the shop floor or in a commercial kitchen? It does not match his social class.' I used to simply laugh at such insinuations. Going to a workplace was therapy in a broader sense and offered Noel a steady source of self-worth. His sense of recognition and acceptance in a difficult social space was an enormous leap in my book. In any case, I had grown up to respect every sort of job in any kind of workplace. Looking at Noel's future in these spaces somehow came very naturally to us.

Pia had set up a nimbu paani stall run by Noel on her

university campus after obtaining permission from the contracted canteen proprietor. Noel sold his nimbu paani at ten bucks a glass, standing alone without shade in the sweltering Delhi heat. It's an image that shall remain etched in my head as I used to often go across to watch from a distance how he dealt with the situation alone. He used to be calm and always greeted his student customers with a wide smile. The good thing was that Noel had perfected pouring liquids into a glass from a jug. It was a line he had crossed over cleanly from the early days of motor coordination deficits.

One important thing to note was that throughout this phase of his work life, in some places, he was remunerated and in others, he was not and got treated as a learner. However, to acquaint him with the concept of monetary compensation for his work, I engineered a salary packet from my side for the jobs he did not get paid for. Noel was happy about getting his salary at the end of the month and the first thing he always wanted to do was to treat himself to a masala dosa!

Noel would never jump out of the car on reaching his workplace. He would wait in the car quietly for nearly ten minutes. Some folks have the ability to instantly adjust to a new environment, social space, new sounds and sights and a different set of faces; that was still not the way it worked for Noel. He needed time to close out on everything that had come before and consciously re-orient and prepare himself for the workplace scenario that he was about to step into. Recognising these needs and always making place for them goes a long way in supporting a child's sensorial equilibrium in our overloaded, complicated life spaces. This might appear to be a small detail but can help the autistic young person in a big way.

———

Learning to travel in the Delhi metro was a big step forward for Noel. After a few trials on the metro, he'd learnt how to use a metro card by himself and navigate his way through the crowds alone (with me, watching him from a distance). No, he never truly travelled all by himself. But he did make progress and was getting there. He often carried a glossy magazine to browse in his hand as a sort of safety blanket, a kind of self-soothing mechanism to deal with the anxiety brought on by the outside world. At twenty-two years of age, Noel had also become adept at asking for a seat from a seated co-passenger since he struggled to remain balanced in the metro.

Once, upon my encouragement, he made a new year's resolution to not ask anyone to give him a seat in case there was nothing available. Just a few days after that, Noel was waiting, with a pensive look, at the Kailash Colony station for the train to arrive. The anxiety bubbled up in his head; what if it was crowded and there was no empty seat? He would have to stand quietly throughout the journey, holding onto something in order to not break his newly made resolution.

The metro arrived and there were no seats available. Noel genuinely tried quite hard to stay fearless while standing in the crowded metro, but his courage ran out in just a few minutes and he began gasping for breath. In the grip of fear, he turned to the row of seats near him and said, 'Mujhey seat dijiye, please (Give me a seat, please).'

He got his seat, sipped some water from his bottle and all was well. But not for me. Noel had acute proprioceptive deficits and so he was unable to maintain proper balance while standing in a state of motion.

The boy had really tried. Seeing him caving in like that made me feel guilty for pushing the seemingly impossible. All of us have physical limits and we must acknowledge that. We do not have to deliver on our resolutions. We need not always win. It is the attempt that is of greater importance.

Many compelling lessons were learnt, all in one moment.

Noel Lights Up Facebook

The first time I gave Noel a general tour of Facebook, he remarked, 'This is a picture book, not a face book, Baba.' His logic was flawless!

I would show him the posts on my timeline. 'See how many people have sent love to you, Noel,' and he would quip, 'I send love back to all of them on Facebook. I will give them all a treat: ice cream from McDonald's!'

My steadily rising Facebook circle had never seen or met the boy. Yet, Noelisms, as coined by my Facebook friends, brought Noel social media fame! What then were Noelisms? They were his perspectives on ordinary happenings, sprinkled with wisdom and pragmatism and they gradually became his trademark.

Noel's mind appeared to oscillate between two extremes: the vertical (logical) thinking side and the lateral (abstract) thinking side. That made Noelisms curiously interesting, charming, goofy and often endearing. There were instances when he tried hard to accomplish something, giving us new insights underpinned by his loveable innocence and exuberance and his steadfast virtue of empathy.

Noelisms often evoked an instant chuckle and a mental note, invariably for us to mull over: 'Where did that come from? Just why did he say that?' There was never an abstract answer but a lateral one, a quirky one, that was enough to prompt reflection.

His followers viewed those tiny everyday life observations through their own interesting perspectives. People began leaving comments that stemmed not just from a sudden awareness of what it is like to raise a neurodivergent child but were also testament to their genuine interest in learning about Noel, his everyday stories and his unique ways of coping. Encouragement, adoration and laughter in the comments, messages and emojis laced every little post. Many joined Noel's journey to discover more about his life and partake in the delight of Noelisms.

Many friends told me, from an entirely different standpoint, that my posts could perhaps trigger ideas in the minds of parents and teachers of disabled children about possible solutions. It could inspire them to try new things, teach their children new vocational skills, or simply let their hair down, relish the present and seek enjoyment in the companionship of their child.

There were more dimensions and meanings in my social media posts than I could surmise!

At home, as Noel stepped into his late teens and moved to his twenties, a characteristic upbeat tone permeated. He was this fountain of love for everybody around, punctuated with an overflowing sense of cheekiness and playfulness. Noel's warmth radiated seamlessly when he entered a room. He would not spare anybody when it came to playing harmless pranks and affectionate teasing, not even the grumpy plumber who, on his occasional visit, would willingly part with his two-wheeler helmet because Noel always wanted to try it on. Then there was the poker-faced office driver whose bulgy cheeks got gently squeezed by Noel as soon as he arrived at the door.

He had a persona that was full of life; his *joie de vivre* lifted everyone's spirits in the most difficult of situations. For this reason, I have always liked to call Noel the Love Warrior.

He had a solidly grounded belief that he was fundamentally worthy of love and acceptance just the way he was. This belief, I am sure, took firm shape by the time he turned seventeen. An inner force had come about that made him supremely comfortable with himself and the way he related to the world.

It is perhaps this self-assuredness that allowed him to overturn some of his fears and deficits in the areas of sensory integration, motor coordination and receptive and expressive communication.

To give readers a sense of what Noelisms so endearingly stood for and why they drew so much traction from people who had never met Noel, here are a few of my posts plucked from many.

———

Facebook post, 3 February 2014

On a misty February morning at Delhi's Siri Fort Sports Club—with not a soul around, Noel and his father go through the rigour of perfecting their forehand shots. Our everyday truth—keep trying! It's not just patience and hard work but also courage. A kind of quiet courage, that does not roar but pushes you gently to do better.

Facebook post, 3 March 2014

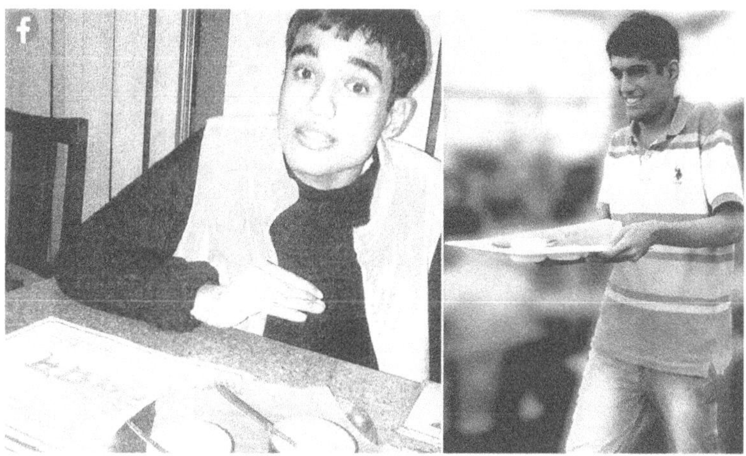

According to this much-travelled young man, the best cuisine in the world is South Indian: paper masala dosa, sambhar, vada, idli and rasam. I guess the combination of simple dishes and tangy accompaniments worked wonders. Very unusual for a *pucca* non-vegetarian Bong, you could say.

Facebook post, 6 August 2014

Noel does not go to sleep until I get home. Rattles me with guilt every time to see this when I step in. Just back from a three-hour delay for a one-hour flight and it's well past 1 a.m. already.

Bleary-eyed, my boy wants to know if I had a good flight!

Facebook post, 14 August 2014

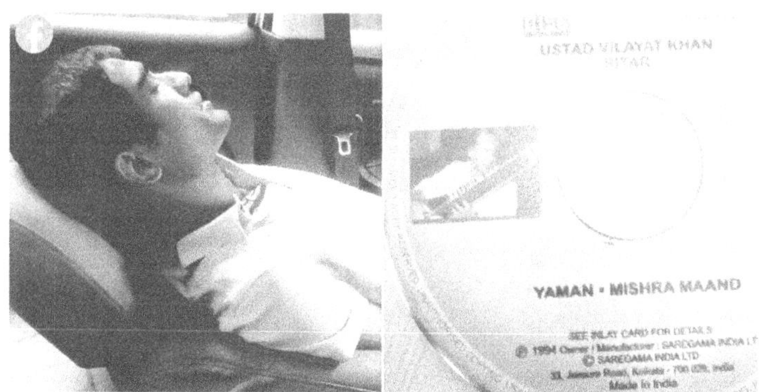

In his early teens, there came a surge in Noel's affinity for Hindustani Classical music—Ustad Vilayat Khan (Yaman, Mishra Maand) and Kishori Amonkar, parallel to his love for *Ekla Cholo Re*, the glorious Tagore song that became popular after actor Amitabh Bachchan sang it on television. Other favourites in his playlist were the Beatles (top favourite was *Hey Jude*), Bob Dylan (*Blowing in the Wind*), Jason Mraz, Deep Purple, ABBA, Shakira (*Waka Waka*), Md. Rafi, Kishore Kumar, Lata Mangeshkar and Salil Chaudhury's Bengali classic *Jhorer Kachey Rekhe Gelam Amar Thikana* (*I Am Leaving My Address With The Storm*) was very special. Amongst his other favourites were also the brilliant Hemant Kumar's rendition of *Runner*, Neil Diamond, John Denver, Billy Joel's (*We Didn't Start The Fire*), Celine Dion (all her songs and, in particular, *I am Alive* and *My Heart Will Go On*). Songs and artists that he warmed up to in his twenties included Taylor Swift (Noel simply adored *Blank Space*), Honey Singh and several songs from the Bollywood movies such as *Love In A Metro* and *Taare Zameen Par*. And of course, a great favourite was the entire soundtrack from *The Sound of Music*. Noel did not care which era a song was from. He was simply drawn in by the melody, the orchestration, the aura and the voice. Audio experiences for him were the biggest high.

Facebook post, 4 October 2014

Burning the effigies of Ravana, Meghnada and Kumbhkarana (characters from the epic Ramayana) depicts the victory of good over evil. It's a part of the celebration of Dusshera. We were in attendance at one such event and in the company of the politicians and other celebrities at Subhash Maidan in Delhi. Small children and people of all sections in thousands were cheering on, thrilled, but Noel was aghast that people could actually revel in the violent act of burning someone (even if inanimate). The incident troubled him greatly. His problem was always with the idea of violence, irrespective of its form. To see people enjoying the decimation of the gigantic human-like figures of the three mythological characters was revolting for the boy and he wanted to leave. I vowed to never again force him to visit a Dusshera show.

I never bought him the typical toy gun that most boys acquire by the age of five for the act of play shooting, be it objects, people, animals or just for fun. I remember I too once had a remarkably real-looking pistol as a small boy, and I had loved flaunting it around as some sort of symbol of power. In adulthood, I became very conscious of this horrific inducement in my boyhood years of mimicking fictional heroes.

Noel was never given a toy gun. Never allowed to see any kind of violence on television or play violent video games. Fortunately, he never understood violence as something to partake in. In fact, he abhorred any bit of violent projection.

I also realised that violence on display or for real as a theme may have absolutely no traction if not seeded in early childhood with fanfare or rewards. In fact, as in Noel's case, in his teens and after, there was only revulsion. His message that day was that symbolic violence is also a form of violence and must be condemned. For him, no excuses for religious traditions or festival rituals should be acceptable to showcase violence.

Facebook post, 26 January 2015

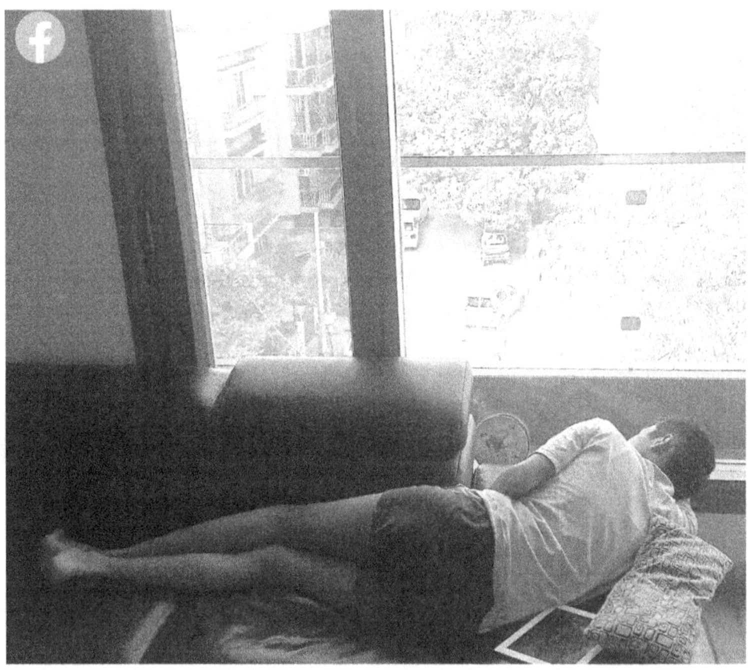

Can a window be a steady companion?

In times of loneliness, sadness and sometimes for the sheer joy of watching birds, trees, fruit vendor carts in the lane below as the day passed by—a splendid colour-filled view from the top— the big window was such a companion. Never will there be a curtain on this window.

Facebook post, 5 July 2015

Sitting in the outdoor café of the club, 'Baba, can you get me a scholarship at Tolly Club in Kolkata?'

'Ha ha! Noel, not scholarship ... membership!'

His expression said it all. It seemed he was convinced beyond a shadow of a doubt that the two were the same.

The golf-loving boy had conflated the two terms, based on the assumption that scholarship and membership are essentially special privileges!

Facebook post, 11 August 2015

Cradling my chin and trying to turn my head ... it is none other than Noel's hand trying to turn my head towards him as he begins to talk.

'if you are listening to me, then you must look at me. Doesn't matter if you are driving. Maybe you can keep saying yes and I will know. It is not enough to listen to another; you must make it clearly known that you are indeed listening.'

A lesson for me. A lesson for all fathers, husbands, bosses, colleagues and all my FB friends!

Facebook post, 29 September 2015

Noel is very fond of old Hindi movie songs and he always tries to sing along to the so-called evergreen ones. The thing is that his key takeaways of the lyrics are often something else—they make me smile but also sadden me at the same time.

It was the turn of that delightful song from the Raj Kapoor classic *Shree 420 (1955)* this afternoon, sung by Manna Dey and Asha Bhosle: '*Mur mur ke na dekh mur mur key ... zindagi ke safar mein tu akela nahin hai, hum bhi tere saath hai ... duniya usi ki hai jo aagey dekhey ... duniya usi ki hai jo chalta jaye ...* (Don't turn back and look ... in this life journey you are not alone, we are also with you ... the world belongs to those who only look forwards ...)'

To my query about the meaning, Noel sums up his single point takeaway: 'When cycling, *mur mur key mat dekhna, bas aagey dekhna, chaltey jaana.*'

Abstract thoughts, non-linear thoughts and metaphors simply slip away from the beautiful autistic mind.

Facebook post, 29 September 2015

Noel loved flipping through magazines to discover pictures that were extremely intricate and busy. He appeared to derive great enjoyment by immersing himself in such images. One such instance to elucidate this is a set of double-spread pictures of the Boeing aircraft factory in the National Geographic magazine—an overview drone shot that was staggering in detail. This would absorb his attention for hours.

The other type of pictures that Noel liked were those that were familiar subjects, with a fun twist. Excitedly, he once told me, 'Baba, see Mona Lisa! She is making a funny face!' It was a cartoon illustration of Mona Lisa, a chubby-cheeked doll, on the cover of the National Geographic Traveller (October 2015—the picture on the magazine cover was a visual metaphor to highlight the lead feature of that issue: 'The Changing Face of Cities'). The illustration showed Mona Lisa swelling up her cheeks. Noel found that hilarious! Also, he liked puffing up his cheeks in the presence of people as well and probably felt that its legitimacy in a social situation was asserted by that picture.

I asked Noel, 'So what's better? A beautiful Mona Lisa or a funny Mona Lisa?'

His prompt reply: 'Funny better!'

Facebook post, 1 January 2016

Fitness is the laudable New Year resolution that father and son make. Noel introduces me to a concept that he has named Half Lunch ... that is, when you have had a heavy breakfast, make sure you have 'half lunch'.

And one more thing he asks me to do: enjoy some cycling in the day or at night ... so then, friends, follow Noel's advice this year and 'stay fit in 2016'!

Facebook post, 1 May 2016

It was Birinder Maggie Kalra's wedding reception, one of Noel's favourite teachers at school. With much anticipation, Noel arrived at the Metropolitan Hotel. The lanky fellow stepped up on the dais and greeted the bride with panache.

'Congratulations! I am happy for you!'

In the midst of the pomp and fanfare, suddenly, he had a flashback from his school days. He said, tearful, 'Birinder madam, my hand is cut, please, can you put a bandage?'

The bride was unfazed and proceeded to shower him with instant attention and care.

Something I have ruminated on is the glorious opportunity to meet some extraordinary teachers with extraordinary temperaments in our journey.

Facebook post, 21 September 2016

I was accompanying Noel. He was part of the contingent at the athletic competition at Thyagaraj Stadium at the Special Olympics (Delhi Chapter). To sit on the comfort of my lap when he was asked to sit on a grassy patch was so natural for the twenty-year-old, 6-footer Noel! It made for a funny scene for the others watching but he could not fathom the hullabaloo about why this was a socially inappropriate thing.

To do what was comforting, what was convenient, what was easier without causing no physical harm to anyone, appeared to be his guiding principle. It did not matter if it appeared funny to others. Being socially awkward in other's eyes never bothered him at all. It stopped bothering me too and the volume of concessions on this count only grew in number as time went by.

Facebook post, 29 January 2018

I had given up the possibility of Noel going any forward on golf skills (an activity that he started at ten and persisted till twenty-one) so it had been struck off from his routine for nearly a year as his interest seemed to wane and progress had declined. One Sunday, the young man, then twenty-five, suddenly persuaded me to take him to the Siri Fort Sports Complex and insisted on going for a 50-ball bucket. With amazing focus, he practised his driving shot. The lesson that he delivered to me was simply this: 'I don't play to compete with any other person. People say about golf being a game that you compete with your own self not always with a player on the opposite side. Baba, I am not interested in competing with myself either ... I play for pure enjoyment, not to improve or compete. Dad, now open your eyes and see the world as I do.'

Facebook post, 30 September 2018

Welcome to a new world. It's called shop floor therapy! That's my coinage. Here, you see Noel who has overcome major eye and hand coordination and fine motor deficits; he is working in a Faridabad export garment factory with considerable dexterity.

Facebook post, 10 December 2018

Noel got appointed to work as a support giver at an occupational therapy (OT) clinic for small children for the evening sessions. It was feasible because he would be back from his day job by then.

The OT specialist had told me that she had observed the young man's caring and gentle approach towards the children and she was impressed. The kids came in for various therapy sessions in the evening—jumping, ball compression, ring throwing and so on.

This picture is a favourite of mine—a highly bemused Noel, when one kid suddenly plonks himself on the lap of the assistant! Baba, what am I supposed to do?

Facebook post, 20 March 2019

Noel with his mother in Manali on vacation.

The fixation with any place where he went for a short trip was extremely unusual after he had crossed sixteen.

Whether it was Goa, Bhopal or Manali, the reaction was the same on the last day. He would be entirely broken as he would be asked to 'pack up'. A story would have to be cooked up to persuade him to get himself together and get ready to leave.

Often, the story would be 'we are not going back to Delhi, we are moving to another beautiful destination to continue our trip'. He knew that it was a piece of fiction after the first couple of times. But the smokescreen worked even after that. It was his assuaging mantra. It unfailingly calmed him down after his initial despair. On arriving in Delhi, Noel would be his cheerful, sprightly self.

In a competitive world that has conditioned people, by and large, to become self-centred and pursue wealth, recognition and fame—a world that had made me exceptionally cynical as a co-passenger in this journey—I was happy to discover a human side that was so palpable and real. A side that was full of appreciation, unqualified love and empathy devoid of any self-agenda. This heart-touching discovery is truly another unexpected gift I received because of my son, Noel. As his dad, they shall remain an invaluable treasure. It did, surprisingly, offset my all-encompassing sense of cynicism—opening the doorway to light and hope forever. It became a healing touch for the innate fragility in my worldview. My faith in human compassion at large was restored, in a much broader sense.

Here are just a few of the treasure-worthy comments and direct messages that I received on Facebook from post to post that are worth recalling here.

One of my ex-colleagues, Akanksha, a young mother entirely unfamiliar with the terrain of autism or disability once messaged me: 'Even though I have not met Noel, I have always felt I have known him in person through your beautiful posts. It was always heart-warming to read about him. There is something so pure in the way he views this unfair world ... he is a ray of hope, an inspiration to trust, to love a little more. Thank you for having introduced us to Noel.'

Gabriel, a senior colleague from my first job, wrote to me: 'I read all your posts about your son, Noel, and I am amazed at his sense of humour, resilience and courage.'

Silvija Jestrovic, professor and author at a British University left a comment: 'I love this boy and always will. Noel's wisdom and beauty will always shine through.'

A professional photographer in Delhi, Amit, left a comment: 'My heart goes out to the brave kid. There is so much to learn from Noel's diary.'

From Sheba, my first boss at the ad agency where I started my career: 'Dearest Noel, you are magical, you bring with you all things good and pure in this world! When I read your snippets at the end of a tired day, you are pure joy. I can only thank your wonderful dad for making all of us a part of your wonderful extended family.'

More comments from some of the remarkable cheerleaders on Facebook, to whom I owe special thanks! They kept me going.

Aurobindo Mohanty: 'Noel for me even if I have never met him has been and will remain an inspiration for me ... there was something divine about him and quite often had words of wisdom to share.'

Subhabrata Ghosh: 'Noel gifted us something far more important than all that we chase. Blessed is his soul.'

Pooja Kohli Jayaram: 'Your son is amazing! I am so deeply inspired by your posts and the pearls of wisdom he drops so casually. Also, beautiful is your compassion and your close connection with him.'

CHAPTER FIFTEEN

Where Is Heaven?

A little-known place but one that promises exhilarating experiences with its amazing collection of cars, buses and various other modes of transport all lined up in one place: The Heritage Transport Museum, which is about 66 km from South Delhi, off the Delhi-Jaipur Highway. In my head, the long drive from home was going to be worth it all. This, then, was one of the journeys of discovery for the dad-son duo. Often on a holiday, Noel and I would set out to an unknown place in and around Delhi.

As we stepped inside the plush museum building, we found wondrous exhibits provided by generous collectors of a wide range of transport vehicles, including century-old traditional modes of transport ranging from the 'palki' (a palanquin, formerly used in Eastern Asia, is an enclosed litter borne on the shoulders of four men/carriers by poles) and horse-drawn carriages to high-tech buses and cars.

A massive collage in one corner was an installation of different vehicular wheels, an old Calcutta tram, truck art of North India, horse carriages, rickshaws and boats, that provided breathtaking views. The final marvel was a sparkling collection of vintage cars that appeared as a sort of grand finale in the last room.

While I enjoyed every moment of the time, I noticed Noel had slipped into a pensive mood and was unusually quiet. He had a pained expression and I simply could not fathom why this was so. I tried cheering him up by taking him into a mock petrol station in the museum and allowing him to be the serviceman by holding the fuel pipe in his hands. I clicked some pictures with him on a daringly small fuel-efficient scooter—a designer's 'concept exhibit'. But nothing seemed to lift Noel's spirits.

After a prolonged state of absolute quietness, Noel broke his silence, 'Baba, they have all become daddus'. My response was an effusive attempt to divert him: 'See Noel, this is such a smart car!' and pointed toward another car.

'Nah! Baba, even this one is a daddu!' was Noel's firm answer. He then added, in an utterly grim tone, 'They cannot perform anymore. It is very, very sad.'

Noel was used to the concept of cars becoming old and becoming grandfathers, so this was not confusing to me. I only understood much later that he was forlorn about how the cars had been left behind, like old persons living in isolation. He was pained by this idea. By the end of the day, he had been shattered by a wave of pathos. 'Their good times are over, they can only rest, nothing else! Baba, all of them ... they are lonely.' The boy could not hold back his tears.

The trip that had started with the excitement of showing him the museum had turned into an unexpectedly sad saga. I could do nothing to alleviate the feeling of pain that occupied his mind. He began to cry uncontrollably and my efforts to pacify him were in vain.

After trying for some time, I withdrew. I felt that I should leave him to navigate the turbulence of his own emotions by himself.

In the days that followed, Noel would enquire at the breakfast table, 'Baba, are you fine or are you old?' in place of a cheery, 'How are you?'

He had seemingly figured out the tribulations of old age. You could not possibly be fine if you were old, according to his newly acquired perspective. It was an honest, pure and realistic concern that he put forth—the existentialist question of ageing and progressing towards death. I had tried to keep it simple for him all along: 'Noel, everyone grows old, dies and goes to heaven.'

Stretched out on the leather sofa by the side of the very large glass window in the living room with a clear view of the sky, Noel used to draw me into talking about old age and death. He often wondered aloud, 'Baba, where is heaven? Is it in the sky?' He had developed a kind of mild obsessive anxiety around the subject.

My terse response often was, 'Yes! Don't ask again and again.' However, Noel's questions did not cease.

'Will you become old? Will you also die? Go to heaven?'

'Yes, yes.' I was mildly irritated as I had answered that question a dozen times in the day and I was busy on the laptop.

'Baba, after you go to heaven, will you come to visit me? Will you come back for a few days? We will have a good time. You can go back to heaven after that.'

Clearly, in his mind, heaven was a place one could pop in and out of when one pleased. Surely, he assumed, a journey to visit loved ones wouldn't be too difficult.

I looked up and wanting to bring this to a close, said assertively, 'Noel Paul, after a person dies and goes to heaven, that person can never ever come back. Have you got it!?' Silence followed. I was relieved.

But after a few moments, he spoke again, 'When you are very old, Baba, will you die?' There was a slight quiver in his voice. I paid absolutely no attention, typing busily on my laptop keyboard.

Suddenly, he declared, 'Baba and Noel, both will go to heaven ... together! I am going with you when you die.'

I threw my hands up in the air. 'Arrey! You will not be old then. You will still be young. There will be so much to do in your life. Why should you go with me, silly boy?' And this time, I laughed loudly.

He answered, 'Because Noel will be scared without Baba ... that is why.'

My laughter came to an abrupt halt. My heart sank.

Noel, Goodbye

Noel's respiratory system had always been vulnerable owing to his condition of allergic asthma. The attacks appeared every year and then, within two or three months, would disappear. Pia and I had tried all kinds of therapies to treat his asthma, including homoeopathic medications from Germany. Every therapy worked, but only for a short time.

The heightened pollution of Delhi during Diwali and its stubborn presence for several weeks after had become an annual feature and in 2019, the treacherous monster took a very ugly shape. The Delhi Government ordered all schools and colleges to be closed after Diwali owing to an unprecedented spike in the levels of pollution and a sinisterly hazardous AQI reading.

On 13 November 2019, Noel had a severe asthmatic attack at home in the early hours of the morning. On his way to the hospital, his life was snatched away. Our love warrior had been ousted from life at the very young age of twenty-six.

Yes, all the beauty and our fountain of love had come to an abrupt end; a brutally unjustified end. I had been in Pune for work, so I had heard the news from Pia over the phone. A part of me had died with him.

We all valiantly grappled with the ensuing trauma and shock. For many months, it seemed impossible to rationally curb the intense pain we were feeling. To cope with the life-altering loss, we left Delhi temporarily.

'As bereaved parents, we are constantly swimming upstream in a death-denying culture that is always looking forward, always trying to move on to the next thing. What we need is space to walk slowly in our new normal even though it's uncomfortable. Finding this space takes years. It takes a lifetime.'

I read these lines recently in a blog post by Jacqueline Doole, an author and bereaved parent who had lost her young daughter to cancer. They resonated with me powerfully. Looking back, I was then in the same zone.

It was in Udaipur, where I stood watching the sunset from the shore, that I felt Noel's presence near me. The tranquil waters of the Bada Lake, encircled by the rugged topography of hills and jagged cliff faces, were an amalgam of contradicting physical features. But amongst these I could feel Noel's breath close to me. The serenity of the blue waters fostered the non-judgemental connection of a confidant.

In those moments, the sights that enveloped me gradually morphed into a shining halo. It was as if a manifestation of my deep love for Noel was taking shape. This vision was supernatural. It brought with it a profound sense of quiet consolation, though I was experiencing excruciating pain inside. A new chapter appeared to have opened up. The trajectory of my grieving had acquired a new dimension.

Noel was with Mother Nature. I imagined him always springing forward to see me, exchanging smiles with that joyful glint in his eyes, signalling through his characteristic exuberance, 'I will be okay, all will be okay, Baba.'

After suffering a prolonged sense of despair for three years, today, somehow, I inhabit a place that has invisible walls, a kind of cocoon where I now live with Noel in my heart, his being palpable every moment. Enveloped in a surreal cocoon, I am constantly reflective of the journey I had with my son and relive the warmth of every single day that we had spent together.

Today, I have unusual experiences when I look up at the morning sun or the moon in the clear night sky. I have never appreciated these sights before as much as I do now. They fill me with divine admiration like never before. When I look at the swaying trees as the wind blows or as I saunter in the greens of the nearby parks and look at the blooms in springtime, I can only see Noel's love-filled face looking back at me, encouraging me to keep going. And every morning, I feel a swell of optimism when I wake up.

Rabindranath Tagore's *Gitanjali*, translated by the legendary poet himself from his Bengali original into English and published in 1912 (awarded the 1913 Nobel Prize in Literature for this work) has been my soothing companion after Noel's departure. The void will never be filled. But on another level, Noel has left a treasure trove of love, beauty and a real, compelling sense of fulfilment for me.

Verse 45 from *Gitanjali* is what appears to reflect my restlessness, my inner churn. It's a situation that brings with it sorrow and the unexpected light to live on, with courage and a smile. Yes, it has been healing me softly.

'Have you not heard his silent steps?
Every moment and every age, every day and every night,
He comes, ever comes.
Many a song have I sung in many a mood of mind, but all their notes have proclaimed he comes, comes, ever comes.
In the fragrant days of sunny April through the forest path, he comes, comes, ever comes.
In the rainy gloom of July nights on the thundering chariot of clouds, he comes, comes, ever comes.
In sorrow after sorrow, it is his steps that press upon my heart, and it is the golden touch of his feet that makes my joy shine.'

Postscript

The pain that he will never come back home shall exist forever for Pia, Ahvana and me, and his near ones. But the beautiful, exhilarating memories shall remain forever.

On the day, Noel was born, his illustrious maternal grandfather, Utpal Dutt, greeted the newly born baby, with the accompaniment of his favourite composer, Beethoven's great composition, the final part of the Ninth Symphony, *Ode to Joy*, on full volume in the music system in the living room.

A moment of boundless celebration for all four grandparents and shall always be a vivid part of my memory.

At the memorial service on 17 November 2019, the same classical piece was played as a tribute to our love warrior, Noel.

In my quiet grief, Tagore's songs have been my invisible anchors. The soulful musical compositions leave me with a sense of profound calmness, enveloping me in melodic tranquillity.

Two of those widely known songs that I reach for rather often have been *Prano Bhoriye Trisha Horiye, Morey Aaro Aaro Aaro Daao Praan* and *Aguner Poroshmoni Chhonyao Praney*.

It's said that it is very difficult to translate Tagore's Bengali lyrics into the English language. We tend to lose the emotional texture, the aura of the song in the translation process. But then reading the translations one does get a sense of the inspiring beauty of these compositions. The following two translations are by Anjan Ganguly.

Prano Bhoriye Trisha Horiye

Brim my heart, quench my thirst
Bestow me with more life
In your world, in your abode
Bestow me with more space
In my wistful eyes
Bestow with more beams of light
In my cacophonic flute
Bestow with more melodic tunes
Oh Master, grind me with more pain
Bestow with more revelations
Blowing doors, breaking barriers
Help me emerge out, liberate me
Bestow me with more love.

Aguner Poroshmoni

Give a touch of the fiery magical stone to my life
Purify me, clarify me, enlighten me
With all severe pain, purify my soul
Uphold my mortal body high, enlightened

English translations from www.geetabitan.com.

Allow me to serve your temple as the burning lamp inside
Let the lamp radiate through my songs
With your petite touch into the darkness
Nascent stars arise glimmering all night
My eyes will not find a dark spot anywhere
It will be light everywhere
All my sufferings would burn and soar skyward.

At their core lies Tagore's message. All that unfolds has to be soaked in and what matters is alive, lighting up others around you, in full intensity, until you die.

Characteristics of Autism for Common Understanding, National Autism Society, UK

Here is an extract from the website of the National Autistic Society, UK (2021) that provides a very useful outline of the condition of autism and the key issues faced in everyday life. It would be a helpful read for those not familiar with the subject.

Social Communication and Social Interaction Challenges

Autistic people have difficulties with interpreting both verbal and non-verbal language like gestures or tone of voice. Some autistic people are unable to speak or have limited speech while other autistic people have moderate to very good language skills but struggle to understand sarcasm or tone of voice. Other challenges include:

- taking things literally and not understanding abstract concepts
- needing extra time to process information or answer questions
- repeating what others say to them (this is called echolalia)

Autistic people often have difficulty 'reading' other people, recognising or understanding others' feelings and intentions, and expressing their own emotions. This can make it very hard to navigate the social world. Autistic people may:

- appear to be insensitive
- seek out time alone when overloaded by other people
- not seek comfort from other people
- appear to behave 'strangely' or in a way thought to be socially inappropriate
- find it hard to form friendships.

Repetitive and Restrictive Behaviour

With its unwritten rules, the world can seem a very unpredictable and confusing place to autistic people. This is why they often prefer to have routines so that they know what is going to happen. They may want to travel the same way to and from school or work, wear the same clothes or eat exactly the same food for breakfast.

Autistic people may also repeat movements such as hand flapping, rocking, or the repetitive use of an object such as twirling a pen or opening and closing a door. Autistic people often engage in these behaviours to help calm themselves when they are stressed or anxious, but many autistic people do it because they find it enjoyable.

Change to routine can also be very distressing for autistic people and make them very anxious. It could be having to adjust to big events like Christmas or changing schools, facing uncertainty at work, or something simpler like a bus detour that can trigger their anxiety.

Over- or Under-sensitivity to Light, Sound, Taste, or Touch

Autistic people may experience over- or under-sensitivity to sounds, touch, tastes, smells, light, colours, temperatures or pain. For example, they may find certain background sounds like music in a restaurant, which other people ignore or block out, unbearably loud or distracting. This can cause anxiety or even physical pain. Many autistic people prefer not to hug due to discomfort, which can be misinterpreted as being cold and aloof.

Many autistic people avoid everyday situations because of their sensitivity issues. Schools, workplaces and shopping centres can be particularly overwhelming and cause sensory overload. There are many simple adjustments that can be made to make environments more autism-friendly.

Highly Focused Interests or Hobbies

Many autistic people have intense and highly focused interests, often from a fairly young age. These can change over time or be lifelong. Autistic people can become experts in their interests and often like to share their knowledge. A stereotypical example is trains but that is one of many. Like all people, autistic people gain huge amounts of pleasure from pursuing their interests and see them as fundamental to their wellbeing and happiness.

Being highly focused helps many autistic people do well academically and in the workplace but they can also become so engrossed in particular topics or activities that they neglect other aspects of their lives.

Extreme Anxiety

Anxiety is a real difficulty for many autistic adults, particularly in social situations or when facing change. It can affect a person psychologically and physically and impact quality of life for autistic people and their families.

It is very important that autistic people learn to recognise their triggers and find coping mechanisms to help reduce their anxiety. However, many autistic people have difficulty recognising and regulating their emotions.

Meltdowns and Shutdowns

When everything becomes too much for an autistic person, they can go into meltdown or shutdown. These are very intense and exhausting experiences.

A meltdown happens when someone becomes completely overwhelmed by their current situation and temporarily loses behavioural control. This loss of control can be verbal (for example, shouting, screaming, crying) or physical (for example, kicking, lashing out, biting) or both. Meltdowns in children are often mistaken for temper tantrums and parents and their autistic children often experience hurtful comments and judgmental stares from less understanding members of the public.

A shutdown appears less intense to the outside world but can be equally debilitating. Shutdowns are also a response to being overwhelmed, but may appear more passive—for example, an autistic person going quiet or 'switching off'. One autistic woman described having a shutdown as: 'just as frustrating as a meltdown, because of not being able to figure out how to react how I want to, or not being able to react at all; there isn't any 'figuring out' because the mind feels like it is past a state of being able to interpret.'

(NAS, UK adds in their official website: The definition of autism has changed over the decades and could change in future years as we understand more)

ASD and Daily Living Therapy, Musashino Higashi School, Japan

A common feature of children with Autism Spectrum Disorder (ASD) is that they are not interested in communicating/interacting with others including parents, especially in their early childhood. They show a strong obsession over certain things and pay little attention to what they are not interested in. As a result, when parents try to help them acquire basic lifestyle habits such as going to the bathroom, eating, changing clothes, and going to bed, they do not accept the guidance and carry out typical inappropriate behaviours that are not seen in TDC (Typically Developing Children). They are often seen by the general public as children with serious disabilities.

In addition, TDC naturally develop lifestyles and grow by following parental guidance and imitating the behaviour of their family members. However, children with ASD in early childhood rarely develop as well as TDC.

Dr Kiyo Kitahara, the founder of MHS, developed a unique educational method called 'Daily Life Therapy®' more than fifty years ago as an educational method for children with ASD who have these characteristics, aiming for their social independence.

Daily Life Therapy® employs a holistic approach in educating the whole child using the three fundamental elements of

- physical stamina building
- emotional stability
- intellectual stimulation

In 'physical stamina building', children establish the rhythm of life by refreshing and physically strengthening themselves through sports and exercise. Then, as their emotional state becomes stable, they gradually improve their concentration and patience. By understanding what is appropriate/inappropriate to do, which is the basis of 'emotional stability', they pay more attention to their surroundings, and their motivation and initiative are fostered. At this stage, they are ready to take guidance on 'intellectual stimulation (development)'; their intellectual abilities are brought out under the guidance of teachers, which further enables them to learn school subjects.

In general, education for children with disabilities tends to focus only on the areas that the target children cannot do, and intensively trains them to correct (remediate) themselves. A similar pattern can be seen in education for children with ASD. On the other hand, Daily Life Therapy® focuses on finding out what the target child can do and helps them develop by observing their behaviour in an integrated manner. If the target child cannot do something, give guidance repeatedly over time. In other words, what is valued is not 'remediation' but 'habituation' so that they can lead their daily lives without much trouble.

Children/students with ASD who are not interested in interacting with others, nor ready to accept guidance will gradually increase what they can do as a result of patient and consistent guidance by parents and teachers and naturally spending daily life with their parents. Along with that, they gradually grow intellectually, become more confident and begin to pay more attention to their surroundings. By establishing their habits over time, there are quite a few cases where they grow up able to adapt to society and engage in daily activities.

Daily Life Therapy® is not an intensive training for 'what they can't do', which tends to put excessive stress on the target child, but helps grasp the whole picture of the child and gradually increase 'what they can do' over time to foster a sense of accomplishment. Based on this Daily Life Therapy®, the school continues to develop more effective methods for educating children with ASD through daily ingenuity.

Appendix Two is an extract from www.musashino-higashi.com.

Acknowledgements

Writing this book for me was an arduous task. I had to overcome my obstinate nature of being a private person. However, the inner driving force of commitments I'd made pushed me through: the commitment towards sharing my learnings with a wider set of parents and educators who I am confident would benefit from this book, my commitment towards making a substantive contribution to raising awareness and understanding about autism in the society at large, and my commitment for honouring the beautiful mind, heart, and soul of our son, Noel.

First, I would like to thank Mr Arun Kapur, a renowned educator, for his encouragement and support of this book from the very start.

In the course of writing this book, I have drawn on several friends for comments on the initial drafts. I would like to thank all of them—my elder sister, Mitali Dutta, and my friends, Brigadier Dr Kunal Ghosh, Chandana Agarwal, Dr Swami Subramaniam (author of Mastering Sleep), Meera Krishnan, Charu Rekha, and Radhika Oberoi (author of Stillborn Season).

My special thanks go to my friends Urmila Chowdhury and Abhiroopa Mathur for counselling me on the publishing aspects.

For permission to reproduce the material drawn from their websites to aid awareness building, I express sincere thanks to two institutions I have always held in high esteem: National Autism Society, UK, and Musashino Higashi School, Japan.

My sincere appreciation and gratitude to Karthika, Sonia, Sanjana, Saurabh, Amrita and the entire Westland team; their enthusiasm and energy have been remarkable!

My wife, Pia (Prof. Bishnupriya Dutt) an amazing mother, and our daughter, Ahvana, a constant pillar of support for Noel, provided valuable suggestions. My heartfelt thanks to both.

www.ingramcontent.com/pod-product-compliance
Lightning Source LLC
LaVergne TN
LVHW050858200726

843508LV00011B/2052